MW00795383

ROAD OF SORROWS,

Life of Joy

ROAD OF SORROWS, Life of Joy

DOLORES DODDS

gatekeeper press™

Tampa, Florida

This book is memoir. It reflects the author's present recollections of experiences over time. Some names and characteristics have been changed, some events have been compressed, and some dialogues have been recreated.

The views and opinions expressed in this book are solely those of the author and do not reflect the views or opinions of Gatekeeper Press. Gatekeeper Press is not to be held responsible for and expressly disclaims responsibility for the content herein.

Road of Sorrows ~ Life of Joy

Published by Gatekeeper Press
7853 Gunn Hwy., Suite 209
Tampa, FL 33626
www.GatekeeperPress.com

Copyright © 2023 by Dolores Dodds
All rights reserved. Neither this book, nor any parts within it may be sold or reproduced in any form or by any electronic or mechanical means, including information storage and retrieval systems, without permission in writing from the author. The only exception is by a reviewer, who may quote short excerpts in a review.

The cover design and editorial work for this book are entirely the product of the author. Gatekeeper Press did not participate in and is not responsible for any aspect of these elements.

Library of Congress Control Number: 2023943030

ISBN (paperback): 9781662942624
eISBN: 9781662942631

Contents

Prologue

"You're worthless! No one wants you or will love you! You're stupid and weak!"

I had heard these words a long time ago. I didn't understand the spirit world then; neither did I realize there was someone invisible that wanted to destroy me. By now I was aware of the enemy's devices, but I felt so defeated and depressed I couldn't fight back. As a mature Christian who ministered God's word in healing and comfort to others, I had experienced the same attacks on myself many times in the past. But now it was too much to bear. It was all so unfair. This was the third time I had gone through rejection by the people I loved.

What was wrong with me? I had tried to do the right thing, but the harder I tried, the less I felt loved.

"It's because you're a failure; you're not lovable. Look, this is your second failed marriage! Even your mother didn't love you. Now you're a disgrace to your whole family!" Satan piled on the mockery. I began to agree with the father of lies—it was futile trying to argue with him. My brain was burning with pain; I couldn't sleep. Hearing that incessant voice I just wanted to die and stop thinking.

"But Dolores, you can't kill yourself; you know that I am real. Heaven and hell are real. Killing yourself won't end your pain; it will just make it worse," the Spirit of God kept pleading with me.

"But, Lord, I just want the pain to stop," I protested. Even though I had always hated drugs and alcohol, I wanted something to take the pain away.

"If you do that, you will never stop; you'll commit spiritual suicide," the Lord said.

"I don't care. I can't live with this pain in my head!"

I went to the store down the street, bought the strongest liquor, and went back to my apartment where I lived alone since my husband had left, with the idea I would drink myself unconscious. I had told no one what I was about to do. I opened the bottle. As I sat down on the couch, a knock came at my door. It was very late at night.

"Who is it?"

"It's me, Mom, let me in," my middle daughter, Tina said.

"Leave me alone. I'll talk to you tomorrow."

She knew from the sound of my voice something was wrong. She knew that I loved my children dearly and would never turn them away. But I was drowning in my sorrow, and selfishly couldn't even think of what this would do to my children.

Okay, Mom, don't be sad. Everything will be alright," she cried.

I knew that not in her wildest dreams would she ever think I would want to kill myself or drown myself in alcohol—this mother who taught her children the love of God, to trust Him with all their hearts. I had known emotional pain before, but this was like a migraine that wouldn't go away unless I cut my head off.

She left. I poured myself a drink. But instead of drinking it, I fell back against the couch for a few minutes, feeling bad towards Jesus. "I'm sorry, this isn't Your fault. You've loved me, but I'm not lovable anymore," I blurted out. I didn't even realize what a contradictory statement that was. Or how deceived I was.

Moments later, another knock was at my door. I was silent. My sister-in-law yelled, "Dolores open the door; it's me."

"I don't want to talk to anyone" I said.

"Just let me in for a moment. I have something to tell you; then I will go," she said.

Knowing Denise, she was not going to leave, so I opened the door. Standing at the door with my sister-in-law was another good friend of hers. I was perplexed as to why this woman was with her at my door so late at night.

As they walked through the door, my sister-in-law said, referring to her friend, "Mary was woken out of a sound sleep, with an urgent request from the Spirit of God. She called me and said we should go over to your apartment. So here we are!" And she looked over at my coffee table with the liquor bottle and full glass sitting there.

I sat down with my head in my hands. She and her friend knew what I was about to do.

"Dolores, you know this isn't the answer," my sister-in-law said as she looked at the bottle. "God loves you—you know that better than anyone. How many times has He proven that to you? Even now, He woke up Mary, who knows nothing about what you're going through, and told her to get you help."

Somehow what she said brought me back to reality, and free from satan's lies. If the Lord would wake someone up that barely knew me, instead of my sister-in-law who knew everything about me and would only come out of sympathy, then He wanted me to know something important. It wasn't that my family and friends didn't love me. It was that He loved me and understood the secret part of my heart, a place where no human could go, a place that only He had been and still dwelled. My Lord was the only one who could heal me.

Thank God for those who have God's Spirit and obey when He says to go! Thank God this friend of my sister-in-law heeded His call! Thank God for my sister-in-law! She had been through so much pain and rejection in her own life, and she knew all about the damaging effects of alcohol. Having alcoholics in her family, including my brother, whom she'd married, she knew what to say to me.

I told them not to worry; I would be okay ... and I knew I would. I thought as I locked the door, "God loves me so much and has been so faithful, He will help me get through this, just as He's done so many times before."

When I thought about what I had almost selfishly done to my beautiful children, I picked up the liquor bottle and glass, and poured the stuff down the sink. I was so disgusted with myself and felt such repentance towards God and my loved ones for acting so selfishly. If I had taken my life or drunk myself to death, I would have broken the heart of the One who died for me. I would have left my children with a sorrow they weren't meant to bear in this life. Instead of faith and trust in God, I would leave them with a sense of hopelessness about their burdens in life. Why would you do this to those who love you? You don't destroy those who trust you with a selfish act, no matter how bad things get.

There is a promise from God that always comes through if you trust Him: "When the enemy comes against you like a flood, God will set a standard up against him." That's just what the Lord did: He stopped the enemy from destroying me by causing a standard of righteousness to spring up within me.

I saw, yet again, how important it is to listen to God's voice and obey Him: it could be a matter of life or death for someone. I was reminded of how satan sets up a plan with the help of people who do not put God first in their lives—like my husband—using them to break you down and then close in for the kill. He tries to destroy two birds with one stone by destroying marriages and your walk with God. I don't care how long you've walked with the Lord and how well you've braced yourself for satan's devices. Satan can blindside you as he did with Job in the Old Testament.

But God is always right there. He knows rejection and unbearable suffering. He has conquered it and won the battle for you. Once you accept that, you are free. It's your choice.

CHAPTER 1

My Young Life

My story begins with the memory of a young girl's first encounter with God. In my little world, it seemed that I was the center of my parents' and grandparents' life.

Maybe I was around three years old that the thought came to me, "Everyone likes me. I am so special. Everything and everyone is made for me."

The next thought didn't come from me, and it addressed me personally. "No, Dolores, I am bigger than you." Funny thing to say to a child! I heard it in a way only a child my age would understand. Somehow with these words, God was letting me know that He was more important than me, and everything was made for Him, including me. This would be the first time I would hear the voice of God and be aware of His existence.

When I was five, I would have my second experience with Him. I loved to play outdoors in the summertime. The grass was green and soft under my bare feet. The large maple trees in our yard looked like green mountains against the blue sky to this little girl's eyes. Summers were mild, always a soft breeze on the clear days. It was the best place to be in America in the summer. My dad was working on his tractor outside. I liked being outside with my dad, and that day was no different.

Our house sat on the only small hill on our property, and I was running up and down the slope leading down from our house. Then I saw some pretty yellow dandelions blowing in the wind. I sat down on the slope and picked a few to play with. I was having so much fun playing, I didn't notice the storm clouds gathering. Only when the sun was hidden by the huge white and gray clouds, and it became darker, did I realize a storm was coming. With the sound of thunder, fear gripped me. For some reason, I couldn't move, and I cried out to the One who was bigger than me. "Please don't let the storm hurt me!" Then I was able to run into the house. That was my second awareness of God, but my first awareness of fear, and I knew I needed the One who was "bigger than me."

That was only the beginning of learning who God was and who I was to Him. At the time, only God knew what I needed to learn and how long it would take to teach me. It would start along the road of sorrows.

This is my story, a story of suffering and redemption. It's an old story going back to creation, and so it is your story too. You may have had different experiences in life, yet we are all sinful, rebellious, prideful people, rejecting the God who created us, and His plans for us. All too often, we try to be God unto ourselves to control our destiny, while all the time the Father is saying, "Child, come to Me; I will give you rest. Come to My Son; I will set you free. Come to My unconditional love, the kind of love you've been looking for all your life. Come, My child!"

Two Different People

I grew up in a small farming community in a middle class household. My dad was a farmer and factory worker, and my mother was a housewife. Life was pretty much the same as all the kids around. I liked the things all kids my age liked: riding my bike and playing outdoors with my brother, who was a year and a half younger than me. We spent a lot of time outdoors—we didn't have a TV at that time. My brother and I would play cowboys and Indians after the few movies we got to see. Our yard was a full acre and there were fields where my dad planted corn, potatoes, and carrots. We would run through the giant stalks of corn, playing hide and seek. Since the woods across the street were denser and hillier, we would cross the street to hunt for arrowheads, which we kept as treasured possessions.

Since I preferred being outdoors to playing with dolls and had only my brother as company, I was sort of a tomboy. I learned to play rough and tough. I used to wrestle with my brother and would always beat him, though one day we were playing football, and he sent me flying over his shoulder, breaking my collarbone! I had to go to school for a week wearing a cast that made me look like a real football player. That ended my football days and beating my brother.

The hill across the street from our house sloping down to a lake was perfect for sledding in the winter. Even though I liked sledding, I hated the cold and having to gear up for the ride. I was not the only one in my family who didn't like the cold. My mother was constantly turning up the heat in the winter, while dad would turn it down. It was harder for my dad to keep the furnace supplied when we had coal heat, but we finally installed a gas heater.

My brother, sister, and dad were always too warm, while Mother and I were always cold. At the time, it seemed like that was the only thing my mother and I had in common. Later on in life, I realized we were alike in many ways that were not good for either. On the one hand, my mother was a very caring person, generous to a fault. On the other, she was controlling, critical, and angry.

My dad was just the opposite. He was a man of few words, but I don't remember him ever speaking a mean word to anyone. He did not like confrontation, especially with my mother. In my mother's case, growing up with nine siblings and being one of the older girls, she had too many chores. With so many children in the family, she also took on the role of second mother to her brother and sisters.

It wasn't easy for my grandparents to raise nine children— just by some of the things my grandmother told me. She said she had to be strict because of so many children. I think somewhere along her growing up years, my mother began to build anger and resentment in her heart. By the time she was married, she had an aversion to housework. She liked cooking but would leave the supper dishes in the sink until the next day. She also enjoyed sewing but would leave yards of material on the dining room table so that you couldn't eat on it. She loved the crossword puzzles in the newspapers, and she would dump stacks of them on the couch so that you couldn't sit on it.

One day I was going to have some friends over. Mother had gone to visit her mother for a little while, and because I was embarrassed about the clutter, I decided to take mom's material off the table, so my friends could sit and drink pop and talk. I sat the material over by the sewing machine, thinking I could put it back on the table later. Mother got home before my friends came. Thank the Lord for that! She was mad at me. "Don't you ever touch my stuff again!" she yelled, taking all the material and putting it back on the table. Believe me, I never did again; nor did I ever help her with anything in our house.

From then on, I tried not to invite my friends over. Children don't over analyze the reasons for things, of course. But when I look back, there were underlying reasons for everything, even though they were not meant to be taken personally. As an adult, I know now mother thought I was criticizing her because of the way she kept house.

My dad's mother was quite the opposite. She kept her house spotless even though she herself raised seven kids. At times my dad's parents would walk across the field to visit us—unexpectedly—as there were no phones, and then my mother would hurry to clear her things off some of the furniture, so they could sit down. My mother knew what grandma thought of her house cleaning skills.

I often wondered how dad could live in such a messy house, but he never complained about it to her or anyone else. One time I asked him about it, and he said, "It's more important that your mother welcomes everyone who comes to our house." I knew my father loved my mother, but I also knew he did not like arguments. Even though he rarely confronted her on anything, she seemed to direct her critical spirit toward my dad and me the most. Naturally, I began to form a close bond with my dad and grew apart from my mother.

At first, I tried to please her, thinking she wouldn't criticize me and would love me if I could do better. As I got older though, there came a time, I decided nothing I did would ever make her love me, so I stopped trying or caring. I'm not sure exactly when, but, over time, not only did our relationship change, but the same spirit she had was forming within me. Anger was building a wall in my heart, and I needed to protect myself from the pain of rejection.

My dad was quite the opposite with us. He would try to give us some work outside, but when we didn't do it, he wouldn't say anything about it. Of course, my brother and I would rather play. Dad was a hard worker. Not only did he keep our farm spotless but would get up at 4 a.m. to do chores, feed the chickens, milk our few cows, and then get ready for his factory job. Whatever dad did, he was devoted to and did well. He was faithful not only to his work, but also to my mother. It took being hit by a car for him to not come home on time; he spent four days in the hospital with some broken bones. Being so young, I didn't understand I could have lost my father through that accident.

Dad had his weaknesses, though. He was insecure about having only an eighth-grade education. In those days, if you were a boy and your family had a farm, you had to help with farm work. As the boys got older, some decided to finish school, but dad loved the farm, and grandpa needed the help, so he quit school. He also had a problem reading.

I found that out one day when I was twelve years old. I came home from school with directions from my teacher to have my parents help me with reading. Mother was in the kitchen cutting up vegetables for dinner. I walked in and said, "Mother, will you listen to me read? I'm having trouble at school reading, and the teacher wants you to help me."

"I don't have time," my mother said.

She could have said, "I'm busy now, but I'll help you later." I wanted to cry but I had hardened my feelings towards her and would not cry in front of her. My mother would never help me with schoolwork or show any interest in my education, even though she had finished high school at the top of her class. I never really understood why my mother wouldn't help me. She was brought up in an era where girls were homemakers, and were not looking to careers.

My father, who was in the basement working on a project, heard me ask my mother to help me read. "Dolores, come downstairs," he said. When I sat down next to him, he asked me to read to him. That was one of my loving memories of my father. Years later, I found out he couldn't read well himself and had turned down a supervisor position in the auto factory because it required paperwork and he was just too embarrassed to have them find out about his reading deficiency.

Because of my father's caring gesture that day, I not only learned to read better, but I began to love reading. It's funny how children's lives are impacted by the small kind things rather than the big events. I didn't need to receive attention 24/7, but I needed my parents to set aside their own needs when it was important.

CHAPTER 2

Lack of Discipline

I was born during World War II. After the war and into the 1960s, the middle class became prosperous. God was blessing both the United States and the Jewish people. Israel became a nation in 1948. God's promise to return the Jews to their homeland in the last days, and the prophecies of the prophets Isaiah and Jeremiah were coming to pass.

My parents weren't wealthy during this period, but we had a comfortable life. My mother wasn't concerned about nice clothes or furniture for herself or her home; yet she made sure we kids were dressed in our best. She gave us money whenever we needed it, without requiring us to do chores to earn it. I would often ask her for money to ride my bike up to the corner drugstore to sit at the counter and order a cherry coke with my friends. She never set any rules for me, so I could come home when I wanted to.

She continued doing things in this haphazard way with us kids even when we began to date and attend parties. This was disastrous for us. I began to feel she didn't care what happened to us. Most of my teen friends had rules or else they would get into trouble. I took advantage of all that freedom. We did what we thought would be fun, and our friends thought we were having fun. But deep inside I felt unloved.

A life without Boundaries

As we got older, fun to us meant parties, dancing, drinking, and, later, drugs for my brother. My brother was a natural athlete and was doing well in his studies. But at fifteen, he began to go out to parties after the football games, and started drinking. At the age of sixteen, he was so good at football he could have earned a scholarship to college, but, partly because my father didn't believe sports was necessary, and partly because he had no rules to follow in his own life, he eventually became an alcoholic. He felt our dad had rejected him, and alcohol would give him acceptance by his peers.

Half the time, he couldn't get up for school on time anyway. His grades dropped, and he was kicked out of football. Mother couldn't bring herself to believe that it all stemmed from lack of discipline. She would blame it on the friends he ran around with or because my dad wouldn't go to his football games. At this, Dad would become quiet because he didn't want to argue with her. I think she nagged him so much, he became very resistant to her demands, which didn't hurt her as much as it did my brother.

Yet when it came down to it, our behavior came from our own choices. We both let anger and rebellion rule us. You may be thinking, wow, their life wasn't so bad? After all, they had a mother and father who were faithful to each other, a mother who took care of them and a father who provided for their needs. These things would be understood and appreciated by me many years later. But my parents couldn't say, "I love you" to us kids because their parents did not say it to them. They didn't show physical affection to us because they had none as children. Their way of showing love was by my mother being there, feeding us, washing our clothes, and making sure we had the material things we wanted. Father provided a place to live, food on our table, and money for our mother to buy us those material things. Their parents used to show their love this way, and they were doing what they knew. Funny how those same parents were now my grandparents and gave me so much love and affection!

Later I was able to understand my parents better. Parents tend to pass on what they have learned from their imperfect parents. Even the best of parents cannot match the unconditional love God provides, so if parents do not have God in their lives, they don't have the wisdom needed to raise children. My parents did not have a relationship with God when they were raising us. Children need more than what my parents thought was love. They need to be told they are loved and shown affection. They need rules, and they need parents to make sure they follow through on those rules.

Children cannot discipline themselves on their own. They learn to discipline themselves by seeing and understanding why following rules helps you make fewer mistakes, and guides you towards a more productive life. Then when they are older, they will choose to discipline their own life. Most of all, they need to learn they need God in their lives to help them make the right choices. If the children have not learned this, it will cause constant trouble for the parents. Later these same children will take that trouble into other relationships they have as well.

When this trouble becomes overwhelming to the parents, they usually handle it in one of two ways. They just ignore the children completely, and throw their hands up saying: "I don't know why they act this way! I don't know what to do with them!" So, they blame the child for their own deficiency as a parent. They may even call Social Services to handle the problem, kicking the child out of their house and getting rid of that responsibility. The other way of handling any trouble is by some parents criticizing or yelling at the child, berating the child for their behavior while continuing to give in to the child's demands.

My mother chose the latter for me. She criticized me and my dad this way. There were times she blamed my dad and others for my brother's behavior. Some parents use physical abuse toward children. Since we are talking about emotional abuse, I have learned that emotional abuse is just as damaging, perhaps worse. My father chose to say nothing to my mother about her verbal abuse of me—very likely because she would attack him too. It hurt me deeply, though. I wanted him to protect me. She would also attack my dad about my brother even if he wasn't saying anything.

Growing up, I never quite understood the difference in treatment toward me and what seemed like favoritism toward my brother, and later my sister, but it was obvious who she favored. Maybe she disliked me because I had become like her—stubborn and controlling. I had developed the very traits

11

I most hated in my mother. To someone that is controlling, the worst relationship is to be with someone else who is the same. It means one must pull back and yield to the other, or there will be a war. With my mother and me, there was constant war.

CHAPTER 3

Filling the Void

The shining lights during my early years were my grandmothers from both my father's and mother's side.

My Paternal Grandparents

My dad's grandparents, who came from England and Scotland, were second generation Americans. By the time I came along, my paternal grandfather, had given my father the remainder of the farmland he had left after selling most of it. Parts of our small town in Michigan had developed on my grandfather's estate, so grandfather's house and ours were close to town. Eventually, the school was built a block away from my grandparents' home and only a few acres away from my house. That was the five acres my grandfather had given dad to build a house and have a small farm since my dad was the only son who liked farming.

I could see the school across the field from my house. All this was very convenient for us kids. We had land and woods to play in, but we were also close to town and school, so as we got older, we only had to walk or ride our bikes there. One of my favorite things to do was ride my bike to my dad's parents' house. Their street was a tree-lined avenue, with small homes and well-landscaped yards, typical of middle class homes of that era.

In those days, people had all that was needed to have a comfortable life. Was it a life of luxury? No, but most paid their bills on time, were not heavy in debt, had savings in the bank, a home they owned, a car or two in the driveway, food on the table, and not two overworked parents like we have today. Was it sometimes tight in these smaller homes, with two to three bedrooms and one small bathroom? The answer is, yes, but usually, the mothers made sure the household ran smoothly, especially with the bathroom situation. In some homes, the bathrooms were outside in those days. Am I saying things were better compared to today? Yes, except for the outside bathroom called the "out house." But generally it meant that parents had less stress to deal with. They could run the home more efficiently and have more awareness and control of what their children were doing. Of course, ours was one of the homes that was an exception.

School was so close by, that one day one of the boys was laughing while looking out the windows saying, "Come and see! Dolores' mother is chasing cows!" Some of the kids, including me, ran up to the window; all were laughing—all except me. The cows had somehow gotten out of our fence. My dad was at his factory job, and there was my mother running after the cows with a stick. Finally, the teacher told everyone to get back in their seats. I was so embarrassed that I wanted to crawl under my desk. Our house and field was the only farm so close to town. I tried to fit in with the town kids whose mothers were thin and well-dressed. Although I was mad at them for making fun of my mother, I felt sorrier for myself.

Freshly-baked rolls

After school, my friends and I would walk over to my paternal grandmother's house. As we drew near to her house, we would smell the aroma of fresh cloverleaf rolls she would make. My friends and I were always invited into her home to have one of the rolls and the freshly churned butter from our local creamery. I can still taste the softness of the homemade rolls and the sweetness of the butter melting in my mouth. The natural ingredients she used made all the difference!

My grandmother on my father's side was so different from my grandmother on my mother's side. She was very English and very proper. Her home was spotless, her dressing impeccable—not a hair out of place. She attended the Methodist church and belonged to the Methodist Bridge Club, though I do not remember either she or my grandfather ever mentioning God. In those days, what you believed was a private matter.

My grandmother was very kind to people, including me. The only time I ever saw her angry was when I was very young, and the object of bullying at the school playground after school. The school bully and a couple of her friends came over to me and began to make fun of my shoe size. They kept calling me "Big Feet" until I started crying and ran to my grandmother's house. This bully's parents lived on the same street as my grandmother, and she knew them, so she marched out of the house, saying, "Come with me!" Grandmother and I went right to the girl's house, knocked on their door, and the girl's older sister answered the door. Grandmother then told her what her sister had done and that she needed to apologize to me. Instead, the sister scolded my grandmother and said, "Old lady, you'd better get out of here!"

The parents weren't home, so my grandmother left. But she told the girl's mother later what had happened, and the mother made her daughters apologize to my grandmother and me. It didn't help change the girl's attitude because she continued to be a bully and got in trouble throughout high school. I didn't fare any better: I would evolve into an angry, controlling victim for many years of my life.

Insults with a Smile

Funny, but my maternal grandmother would have to face the same situation when I was a young teen. She lived on the other side of town. Next door to her house lived a family that were the village troublemakers. They had two boys, one older to me and one younger, who were mean and always looking for trouble. One day I was on my way to her house on my bike when the older boy came running up to me with a fishing pole and knocked me off my bike, bloodying my nose. He laughed and ran into his house. I pulled my bike up to my grandmother's driveway, blood and tears running down to my chest. She was so upset. As she was cleaning me up and checking to see if I was hurt anywhere else, she said,

"I would go to his parents, but it wouldn't do any good. They are worse than their boys." Poor grandmother! And she lived next door to them all her life!

The story told about my maternal grandmother through the years is still cloaked in mystery. She and my grandfather had come to this country as young adults from Austria. They met, married, and settled in New York before coming to Michigan. We were told she could speak up to six different languages, and that while she was in New York, she had a job with the U.S. government as an interpreter for people applying for citizenship. I don't know what job my grandfather had then. No one talked about it, and since he died before I was born, I didn't think to ask. Our parents told all the kids in our large family that our grandmother was from Hungary or Yugoslavia. They also said grandmother was an only child and had brought some furniture and art pieces from her country of origin. It's a wonder how they managed to load that on an immigrant ship bound for America during the war!

Years later, I learned through my research on the internet and from documented records that both my maternal grandparents were born in Austria. Grandfather lived in a couple of other countries, and grandmother's parents moved around a lot to different countries—which could explain her ability to speak so many languages. I also found out that my grandfather had decided to leave New York where so many immigrants were competing for jobs, and move to our small town in Michigan where he had more opportunities for enterprise. He opened a car repair garage and later purchased some homes in the city to rent out.

A relative told me that when they moved to this town, the people treated my grandmother terribly. If she were walking on the same side of the street as they, they would move over to the other side. Some people in town even burned a cross in the park across the street from my grandparents' home. Since no one in our family explained or seemed to know why this happened, I thought it was because my grandmother had a dark complexion and had come from Eastern Europe. Most people who settled in this town were from England and Scotland, and had light complexions. There was a lot of prejudice towards blacks, Jews, and certain nationalities. I was told about it after my grandmother died. It made me so mad because she was such a kind person. She would just smile at the people who snubbed her.

Much later in life, I learned my grandparents had probably faced this kind of persecution long before coming to the United States. But thank God, He brought them here because I don't believe they would have survived or that I would be here to write this story. I also believe that my grandparents' grim experience in Europe was the reason why I never heard a bad word from my parents or grandparents toward another race or nationality. As I got older, I heard other people, especially kids, call people of different ethnic backgrounds all kinds of names. Through some research I found that their last name was Jewish. But Grandmother kept all this from us because she didn't want her family to experience what they had been through in Europe. My mother told me my grandmother was Catholic, but that was strange. She didn't go to the Catholic church. When she was dying, my mother had asked for a priest to come, but he never did.

I believe my grandmother kept a lot of secrets from her children to protect them. Many times, when I would stay overnight with her, she would talk to me about God. She was the one who sparked my interest in the God she spoke of. There was something about her that made me want to be near her when I was emotionally hurting. I know now, it was her love for God—how real He was to her. I think it was probably true when she told my mother that she didn't have any relatives left in the countries she lived in. Any of the Jewish people who could not escape these places were put to death in extermination camps.

As the years passed, people became more accepting as different nationalities moved into our town, although it didn't grow much. My maternal grandfather did well. He bought some land in town on a small lake and built a sizable ten-room house for his big family. He was one of the few people in town that had such a large house. He died young, but grandmother lived to be in her seventies. I can't remember her ever going to a doctor or taking medicine when she didn't feel well. She just treated herself with herbs from her garden and natural remedies she had learned in her country.

Why Did They Have to Go?

One day my mother came to my school and removed me from class. We walked the short distance to my father's parents' house and on the way, she told me my grandmother had died suddenly. I started to cry but, instead of consoling me, my mother said, "You need to stop crying; you're going to upset your grandfather."

I stopped crying, but I thought, "What did she mean?" I had just lost one of the two people I could trust with my feelings, someone who understood me. I could no longer go to her house, enjoy the pretty little clean and orderly house, and the smile on her face as she took out the yeast rolls with their wonderful aroma from the oven. No longer would my friends and I enjoy her interest in our lives and school days. How could I not cry?

The day before, she had been healthy but had a pain in her leg. She decided to see a doctor the next day. There were two doctors in our small town, one who had practiced for years, who had delivered most of the babies in town. He would visit your home if you were too sick to leave. The other one was just out of medical school doing his internship. She decided to go to the new one. He examined her and sent her home with the instructions to lie down in bed and prop her leg up. As soon as she got home, she followed his instructions, not knowing a blood clot in her leg had caused the pain. My family told me that doctors did not know a lot about blood clots then or how to treat them. Once her leg was up, the clot traveled to her lungs and killed her.

Anyway, I wasn't allowed to show any emotion, and it didn't matter to Grandpa either because no one could console him. At the burial, he threw himself on the casket as they lowered it to the ground. "Why her? Why didn't I go first?" he cried. My pretty healthy grandfather gave up after grandma's death. He didn't want to live. Within a year, he made himself sick with grief and died.

At thirteen, I lost my Jewish grandmother as well. It seemed she too had never been sick. One day my mother told me and my brother she was bringing grandmother to our house because she was very ill. Mother put her in their bedroom because it was the only bedroom on the first floor, which made it easier for mother to take care of her. The week she came to our house, the doctor visited two or three times, but she wasn't getting any better. I can't remember why she didn't go to the hospital, but knowing grandmother, she probably refused to go. At the end of the week, the doctor told my mother she should call all our family as she would not make it through the weekend.

I don't think he knew what made her so sick, but he told my mother she was dying of old age. She had a big family, and they all came to see her one last time. They were all so somber; mother had asked that they go in one by one to spend a little time with her and say their goodbyes. My brother and I were the last ones to go in. Mother knew how much grandmother meant to us, and she also knew it would upset us. I had already been crying all day when she said my grandmother was dying, but she wanted us to spend a few minutes with her and say goodbye. I didn't know what to expect, but I believe God wanted me to see someone who trusted in Him pass from this life to eternity.

She was lying there with a peaceful look on her face as my brother and I sat down by her bedside. She had not said a word for a few days, and she did not say anything to us, but that peaceful look on her face said, "I will be okay; I'm not afraid." She just took our hands, smiled at us, and fell asleep in Jesus. After becoming a Christian, I realized that she wasn't afraid because she knew her Savior, and she knew where she was going. After she took our hands and smiled, she closed her eyes. There was a slight rattle in her throat, and her spirit left her body.

I would remember how she died all my life. This time no one was going to stop me from crying. I grieved for over a year and missed her so much, it hurt. Now I had no one to calm my hurt, no one to talk to. After I lost my second grandmother, I became angrier, especially toward my mother. My life would begin to pick up speed on the road of sorrows.

CHAPTER 4

The Search for Acceptance

The troublemakers in town were mainly kids who were allowed free rein like I was. So of course I began to spend more time with them. At first, I got involved in social life in school and wanted to be with kids in sports and made good grades. In the eighth grade, I even tried out for cheerleading.

Quick Prayer

I practiced hard to win a spot, but when the teachers announced the names of everyone on the team, I had not been chosen. Right that moment, I asked God, "Make me a cheerleader, please." I wasn't pleading, but in shooting a prayer to God so quickly, I didn't have time to look at the impossible circumstances. The fact was the cheerleaders had already been chosen. I didn't have time to doubt: I just wanted to be a cheerleader. Being a young girl, not knowing anything about God except He existed, I believed He could do anything.

I don't know why I turned to Him, but I think the Lord wanted to teach me in the way He responded that there is nothing impossible for Him. What happened next completely floored me. One of the teachers said, "Just a moment, we have a problem." The teachers then left the gym and said they would be back shortly.

We all waited on the bleachers, wondering what was wrong. A few minutes later, they came back and announced they had mistakenly chosen two girls from the same family, which was against school rules. So, they would have to give the position to the next person on the list. That person was me!

God was teaching me what He could do if I believed in who He was and, most importantly, that He cared for me. Since I didn't go to church, or had close Christian friends, I prayed only when I was desperate. I didn't read the Bible much, and moreover, I didn't understand what I was reading. I didn't know what was required to have a full relationship with God. I soon forgot what He had done for me and went on my not-so-merry way, walking toward the darkness.

I remained a cheerleader until the middle of my sophomore year, when I was kicked out because of my low grade average.

Between the age of twelve and eighteen, I tried to find out more about God at different times. A couple of girls invited me to their church, so I went to a Sunday service with them. The young people all sat clumped together. They didn't seem interested in the Pastor's sermon and they just gossiped about each other and passed notes. I didn't get anything out of the sermon either; he kept quoting from everywhere except the Bible. I thought this was no different from school. The kids didn't seem to have any respect for God, and the Pastor didn't even seem to know God. I didn't go back.

There was also a small Catholic church down the road from our house. I watched movies about nuns and heard they did not get married; instead, they would commit their lives to no one else but Jesus. I too decided to marry Jesus because of a yearning to be committed to God. I went to the Dime Store and bought a fake wedding ring, rode my bike up to the little Catholic church, planted the ring behind a bush outside the church, and said, "Jesus, I am now married to You." Nothing changed after that though, and I continued to stay out late and go to parties.

After a while, I got sick of all the drinking and fighting at these parties. But I didn't end up out in a car having sex like many girls; in fact, I still had no interest in boys romantically. I didn't drink or take drugs either because I wasn't going to let anything control me. I had seen enough of some of the relatives on my mother's side of the family ruining their lives because of alcohol. I hated the effects of alcohol, though my shy brother said it helped him have a good time. It made him bolder and feel accepted and loved by all his friends.

I was different from my brother in that sense. I was an extrovert with an attitude. I wasn't intimidated by people, or try to do something just to be liked by others. When I was around fifteen, I decided I would clean up my life and stop going to these parties where everyone had to get drunk to have a good time. In fact, I was not going to hang out with these kids at all. So, one weekend when my mother and father were going out of town to visit some relatives, I saw this as my chance to get into social life with some of the "good" kids. I had made friends with a lot of these kids when I was a cheerleader so, even though I didn't run around with them,

I was still on friendly terms. I also dressed well, thanks to my mother, as that helped make you popular.

So, I called a bunch of kids—cheerleaders, those in sports, and those who made good grades, everyone but my rowdy friends. I would serve desserts and soft drinks, but no alcoholic beverages. We would play music and dance, which everyone liked to do, in my parents' large living room. I was surprised that so many kids showed up, surprised because I was already starting to have a bad reputation as a party girl, running with the wrong crowd. But they respected my parents as decent people and probably thought they would be home.

At first, the party went well; everyone was having a good time. Then out of the blue, two of my rowdy friends crashed my party, already drunk from drinking earlier in the day. Here they were at my kitchen table drinking beer. The kids' scared faces watched from the living room. Embarrassed I said, "Take your beer and leave."

The two brothers just laughed at me and said, "Are you going to make us?" Something snapped in me and the kind of anger that had been building up over the last few years rose up. For some reason, when I would get that angry, I wasn't afraid of anyone. The older brother was a large muscular kid, who was older than me. He would fight at the drop of a hat.

Again I screamed, "Get out!"

"No!" he retorted. There was a bottle of beer sitting next to him on the table. Without even thinking, I picked it up and smashed it on his head. He fell back against the sink, dazed, blood running down his head. His brother called me every name in the book. I didn't care. I just kept screaming at them to get out. I believe only God protected me that day. I know

26

those two were capable of beating me up or even killing me. I had heard some bad stories about them. Some people even thought the older brother was mentally ill.

Then, all of the sudden, the older brother said to the younger, "Let's get out of here." They left but weren't through with me yet. They called our local funeral home, which doubled up as an ambulance station. "This young girl is having a breakdown," they told the dispatcher.

As I apologized to my guests who by now were leaving, here comes the ambulance into my driveway, thankfully, without the siren on. It was serious since I had hit the boy over the head with a bottle. Still, I felt I was the victim, not realizing no matter what these boys had done, that uncontrollable anger could have injured the boy severely. So, they put me in the ambulance and took me to the hospital.

My parents arrived home shortly after I left, as my brother had called them. They came to the hospital after picking my brother up. He had told them the whole story. After they talked to the doctor, he said they could take me home. There was nothing wrong with me, and that the boys had pulled a prank on me.

Instead of apologizing, I said to my mother as I got into the car, "I'm not going back to school." My father didn't say anything, but I knew he was disappointed in me. They didn't punish me for having the party behind their backs. I think my mother felt I had already been punished, which was true. I felt sorry for myself. How would I ever face the kids at school again? It was all about me. I stayed out of school for two weeks, but this was one time my mother put her foot down and made me go back to school.

Facing my peers after something so embarrassing seemed unbearable, but I wasn't about to let anyone see any weakness in me. At first, when I came back, all the kids at the party kind of ignored me. I had a couple of friends, who were in the cheerleading squad and stayed out of trouble, talking to me. I sat at lunch with them in the cafeteria. I acted as if nothing happened, and the kids soon forgot. I guess they were tired of talking about me. Inside though, I was still so angry, and the only lesson I learned was that I didn't fit in with the so-called good kids at school.

So, I focused on having a good time. I fell in love with dancing, and no longer had an interest in any other activity at school that required me to keep my grades up. I became very good at dancing and didn't lack partners. Rock and roll was the music of the day and made for great dance music. Our town had a community center that held dances on weekends. I would drag my brother along since he enjoyed dancing too. I had my license to drive, but he didn't yet.

He also liked to ride up to the Drive-in Restaurant in the city with me to get a hamburger. All the kids from various high schools around the city gathered there. We would sit in our cars with rock and roll blaring from our car radios, eating and talking through our open car windows to each other. How we heard each other, I will never know, but we were young. Since kids from rival schools in sports were there also, this would often lead to fights. The boys would get out of their cars and begin a fistfight; then the owner of the drive-in would call in the police.

My brother was very muscular—the typical good-looking tough guy. But with him, looks were deceiving because of his distaste for fighting. One night as we were cruising through the drive-in on a balmy summer night, a kid yelled out from another car to my brother, "Hey, you wimp, are you a chicken?"

Up to that point, my brother took a lot of abusive talk from guys from different schools, even though they knew he played football for our school. The boys had parked right beside our car. But something snapped in my brother that night. He jumped out of the car before I could say anything and ran over to the other guy's car. "Get out," he yelled.

I think it took the guy with the big mouth by surprise. He just stared at my brother for a few seconds, then jumped out of the car, knowing he had to meet my brother's challenge or look like the chicken he had called out. This kid was about two years older and a foot taller than my brother. But my brother was like a madman.

The minute the kid got out of the car, my brother didn't say a word. He just jumped on him, and beat him to a pulp, before his friend and I could pull my brother off. My brother got back in my car. No police came; he didn't have a scratch on him, but the other guy was bleeding through his nose and had cuts and scrapes from the pavement on his arms and face. They got in their car in silence and left.

That was the night my brother made up his mind he wouldn't take abuse from anyone anymore. What's more, if he felt someone else was being abused or bullied, he stepped in. The trouble is when he drank, he sometimes imagined people were rejecting him. and he would become violent towards them when really they weren't against him. But there were people that loved him and wanted to help him.

But, the truth is, that anger came from a demonic spirit that had overtaken both my brother and me. Anytime I felt people disagreed with me, it made me think they were rejecting me. I know now it had to do with my sense of rejection caused by my mother's words growing up and my brother feeling dad had rejected him. You have only your parents' attitude toward you to frame your feelings about yourself. The trouble is you will surround yourself with like-minded people who react the same way as you. It's like the blind leading the blind.

In truth, our parents weren't rejecting us. They just didn't have the concept of what real love is, only what they had experienced in life. God is the very embodiment of true love, but they didn't know Him or have a relationship with Him. So how could they pass that kind of secure love on to us? If they had a relationship with God, even though they made mistakes in parenting, the Spirit of God would have been there to correct them and teach the parent and child how to forgive. It would take me a few more years to understand this—a few more miles down my road of sorrows.

My brother and I graduated high school by the skin of our teeth. I had wanted to be a social worker and help kids who felt like I did, but I knew my grades were terrible. I also knew my parents would not help me, and I didn't have the discipline to work my way through college. My greatest dream was to go to Hollywood to be an actress and dancer. I acted in a few plays in high school and read excerpts from dramas like Anna Karina in class. The teacher said I had a natural talent, and under my yearbook picture, the book committee put, "On her way to Hollywood."

I knew for sure I wanted to leave this small town and live in a large city. I had some friends who had graduated earlier and moved to Chicago, who would come home for Christmas and tell me how exciting Chicago was—lots of jobs, and so much to do. All I knew about Chicago in my high school years was from the gangster movies of the Al Capone era. They would glamorize the characters in the movie, instead of portraying their lifestyle as evil and destructive. And I got carried away by all that. All I could see from these movies was that the men were bold, self-assured and handsome, and the women were beautiful and led exciting lives.

I left for Chicago thinking I would be a part of a big movie. It's a fantasy many girls and boys have, which gives them no direction in life. What a joke! What a lie!

CHAPTER 5

City Lights

My parents gave me money for a bus ticket and to stay at the YWCA, plus money for food for a month. My friends that were living in Chicago had already let me know what I would need. I was a little worried about finding a job, because I hadn't paid attention in school, and the subjects I was good at, government, history, social studies, would not help me much. I couldn't even type well enough to get a low-paying office job; plus, I thought I was too good to work as a waitress.

The two subjects I needed were math, which I hated, and spelling. I always knew if I applied myself, I could do well in my studies, even the ones I didn't like. But I just hadn't wanted to, and no one at home seemed to care. Till reality hit, all the playing around in school did not prepare me for the real world.

As I rode into the city on the bus and looked at all the tall buildings, then pulled into the bus station with lines of buses and so many people milling around, I felt overwhelmed. Maybe I had made a mistake, I thought. What on earth was I doing in a city this large, with just blocks and blocks of concrete? I didn't have much time to worry about it, though, because one of the girls I knew back home had come to pick me up. If she hadn't been there, I probably would have gone back home.

My friend dropped me off at the YWCA. "You are going to love the nightlife here," she said. That got me so excited. The thought of so many night clubs and bands to dance with was all I could envision. Instead of seeing myself continuing down the slippery slope in that sinful, immoral lifestyle, I thought, "How cool!"

At the YWCA, we had to have a roommate because there weren't many rooms. My roommate was a girl from Wisconsin. She had come to Chicago to get a job and go to school. She was studying to be an x-ray technician. "That's what I need to do: go to school," I figured. Those who had the most education got the better jobs, but first, I had to get a job myself. My roommate said there was a position opening at a place that made parts for the space program. I applied for an office job there and was hired. I worked in filing, which wasn't hard for me to learn, but it didn't pay much. If I wasn't living at the YWCA, I wouldn't have made it. Since the job was in a town just outside the city, I had to find a ride. I took a taxi for a few days, which was too expensive. Unfortunately, the bus didn't serve that area. I asked around at work and found a girl that didn't live far from me in the city. I helped her with gas and rode to work with her.

I liked the job and the people I worked with. If I hadn't been so interested in the nightlife, I could have worked my way up to a better position with more pay. Not only was my work ethic lacking, but I still didn't realize that staying out

33

late and getting up early for a job was not going to work any more than it had at school. Even though it affected my job performance, having fun was more important. I just wouldn't be disciplined. Instead, God would allow things to happen in my life to change my direction.

Less than a couple of months into my new job, I began to experience a lot of pain in my stomach. Even though I had been constipated for days, I let it go because this had been normal for me since I was very young. That reminded me of a strange thing that happened to me at seventeen. I had not had a bowel movement for a week and I was in terrible pain. My mother took me to the emergency room. The doctor decided to give me a colon test with a scope. After they finally got my bowel cleaned out, they gave me some Valium to relax me before the test. After the medication, the next thing I knew, I was above my body, watching them work over me.

I heard one of the nurses say, "I can't get a pulse." I didn't have any fear. I was just amazed that my body was on that bed. I looked down the hallway from the emergency room. From above, I could see everything that was going on. There were a couple of doctors now in my cubicle. One of the nurses put a machine against the wall, which was the last thing I saw. I heard the same nurse finally say, "I got a pulse." I heard a whooshing sound, and I was back in my body. I know that most people will think that it was the drug that had this effect on me, but I'm sorry, there's no possible way I could have seen down the entire hallway with my body lying on the bed while they tried to revive me.

The Mother Superior, an administrator of the hospital, told my mother they had lost me for a moment. She explained that the Valium was a little too much for my system. For me, it felt like time had stopped.

A priest came to my room later in the day. I decided to tell the priest what had happened to me. After listening to my story, all he said was, "That's nice!" I could tell he didn't believe me or thought it was the drugs. I was hoping he could explain why it had happened, but he didn't seem to want to talk further or even pray with me. After that, I decided I was not going to tell anyone—not even my parents. It would be years before I felt I could reveal to anyone the time God had supernaturally intervened in my life in the emergency room.

It wasn't only the priest that had a hard time believing in a spirit world or a God that performs miracles in this generation. There was so much unbelief, even in the church. We no longer lived in the days of the early church, when people knew and expected God to manifest His presence through miracles, healings, answering what was impossible to man, but possible to Him.

No longer was it acceptable to say God spoke to me, healed me, or protected me, or that the Holy Spirit guided me, Jesus is my friend, and God is my father. America had intellectualized God out of our everyday language. There was no satan or his demons; no spirits that possessed people and destroyed their lives. Instead, they had a mental problem that counseling and drugs would fix. Don't get me wrong: all mental health issues are not controlled by demons; but many are. We just give drugs to people to quiet them or shut them away from society. Of course, this doesn't cure them. There are no longer angels that watch over us; there is no hell that God made for the devil and fallen angels, or heaven that believers go to. There is no after life. We are just creatures that appeared out of nowhere by whatever theory some scientists made up with fragmented evidence.

In the sixties, most of the church believed in a God that could only perform natural not supernatural things—which is not God at all. Pastors and priests didn't want to be accused of being delusional. So, they began to adapt their message for more intellectual minds rather than for man's spirit. When I talked to the priest, I thought to myself, "If he doesn't have the answers about what happened to me in that hospital room, who does?" So, for a while, I, too, learned to keep quiet.

I entered my adult years during the most volatile time in America. After World War II, America became very prosperous, which, I believe, was because we had taken the right side in the war, and we were sending missionaries all over the world. God was indeed blessing us. However, when God would prosper Israel, the Old Testament tells us that they would turn to idols instead of being thankful. Just like Israel, America would not be grateful for her advancements and instead raised up other gods to worship. Their names were wealth, power, and materialism. Then, in the seventies, the children who had been raised in the shadow of materialism decided to go a step further and make gods out of themselves. They would glorify the flesh. Now it was all about doing what made you feel good: sex, drugs—whatever. The hippie generation called it "free love." Free love destroyed many people and changed America dramatically.

This was the generation in which I came of age. Moving to Chicago, I soon strayed from my desire for God in my life and joined the rest of America in my selfish desires.

I wasn't long in Chicago before the constipation issue came up again. I ignored it. I was having too good a time going out and partying, not getting enough sleep, or eating right. One day I came home from work and passed out in the hallway of the YWCA. One of the girls saw me and called an ambulance. I ended up in the hospital for three days while they cleaned me out with enemas. I had tests done, but they didn't find anything. I didn't have insurance, plus I had missed three days of work. Fortunately, my parents paid the hospital bills.

I thought, "Oh great, I'm here to make money, and instead, I'm calling my parents for money." Of course, that didn't stop my selfish lifestyle. I got way into the city nightlife, going to clubs to dance sometimes four times a week.

There were many young people like me at these clubs just wanting to have fun, but there were also a lot of shady characters. This was Chicago—gangster land. They all wore expensive suits and flashed around lots of money. Young impressionable girls hung onto them. It's weird, but I thought those girls were stupid. I didn't think anyone should be given that much attention; to me, it was embarrassing. Anyway, I was just there to dance, not meet anyone. I still wasn't interested in dating. But this guy was cute and would always ask me to dance. After a few weeks of clubbing, he asked me out. I said no, but he kept asking, and I thought, "Oh well, why not?"

So, he picked me up that following Saturday for a dinner date. He drove up to the Y in a Cadillac. Some of my friends there said, "Wow, he's got money!" He opened the car door for me, which I thought was nice and he was so handsome.

We went to the most expensive restaurant in Chicago. I ordered steak, knowing on my paycheck that steaks would be few and far between. After dinner, he wanted to go for a ride. He had been an absolute gentleman so far, but I had to be in by midnight, and it was already ten-thirty. "I'll get you home in time. I just want to show you something," he said. I felt uneasy but thought if he gets me home on time, I'll be okay. Girls, listen to your instincts. Instincts are God trying to warn you.

He kept on driving, and at one point, he tried to put his arm around me. He had to reach because I wasn't sitting that close to him. His coat was unbuttoned, and when he leaned over, I saw a shoulder holster on his chest with a gun in it. I moved farther to the door. To think how stupid those girls at the club were, but now I was one of them! I knew nothing about this guy. I didn't even know what he did for a living.

"I want to go home," I said.

"We're already here," as he pulled into a cemetery.

"Oh my God, what are we doing here...?" I gasped.

He drove up to this marble stone, stopped, and got out to open my door. "Come on. My best friend was killed a couple of weeks ago," he said. I thought he was crazy. I walked up to the gravesite with him, and I could see the tears forming in his eyes.

At first, I didn't know what to say—I mean, who does this? I didn't know the dead guy. I didn't even know the guy I was with. Finally, I said, "How did he die?"

"Some people shot him, but they were taken care of."

"What have I gotten myself into," I thought. "He's out of his mind!" This wasn't a movie anymore; it was for real.

"I need to get home. I will be in trouble if I'm late," I said. To my surprise, he just said, "Okay."

We got in the car but I didn't say a word to him the entire way back. He seemed irritated with me. I didn't care. As soon as he pulled up, I jumped out, and he sped off. I told my roommate about it, and she said, "He must be crazy. Why would he think you would want to see a gravesite and hear about his friend's death on your first date?"

"I don't know; I'm just glad nothing else happened to me. I'm not dating anyone here unless I know everything about them. That was so scary."

All things considered, I just wasn't meant to live in Chicago. After a while, I almost began to feel there was a target on my back for bad things. But it wasn't over yet. A couple of months later, a boy from my high school in Michigan asked my roommate and me if we wanted to go to a New Year's Eve party. There would be music and dancing, so that would be a yes for me. He was picking us up. Although I knew he drank occasionally, I didn't expect him to be drinking before the party; but he showed up intoxicated to the point he was slurring his words.

Reluctantly, I got in the car and sat in the middle with my friend next to me. The minute I got in; I could smell the alcohol. I was alarmed and asked him if I could drive. He said he was fine, and drove off. I kept asking him to stop and let me drive. This irritated him, and he began to drive faster. It's surprising how people feel they are always able to control every situation. We may be in control of ourselves, but we're not in control of others. I would learn this lesson over and over throughout my life. People have a will and when they give that will over to the demons of alcohol, drugs, anger, sex, money, and power, they can do significant damage to other human beings.

Back then, if I had been God, I would have attacked someone who tried to harm another person because my anger was so deep-seated against any kind of injustice. I didn't realize that God shows mercy to all His enemies and gives them a chance to repent. He provides the offender the time to repent and ask forgiveness, just as the victim has an opportunity to repent of the hate they have for the offender. Why would He do that? Because if He hadn't, there would have been no hope of reconciliation for any of us. We would go on returning evil for evil.

My friend and I were scared. I had just turned eighteen. I didn't even think to pray. I was just focused on what the driver was doing and kept thinking of ways to stop it. The house we were headed to was out in the country on a twisting desolate road. He had been down this road before. "This road has a sharp curve on it that's called Devil's Curve because there are so many accidents and deaths on it," he said.

I think he was trying to be funny and scare us, but as we approached the curve, I begged him to slow down.

"I can make this curve going a hundred miles an hour," he said as he floored the gas pedal. As we rounded the curve, the sharp turn made his hands jerk off the steering wheel. I tried to grab the steering wheel. It was too late! Before I could blink, we were off the road. The car rolled and landed on its side in a deep ditch. In a split second, I bent my head and body down to not see what was going to happen.

As I did that, I heard an audible voice say, "You won't die yet." I knew it was God, and I knew I wouldn't die in this accident. Later I would think about that voice speaking to me, knowing without a shadow of doubt it was God. It was another God moment I didn't tell anyone about.

A policeman arrived at the scene. Neither the driver nor my friend was hurt, which was a miracle considering the state of the car. I didn't feel anything, not even pain. I didn't realize I had been hurt until I noticed blood dripping from my head onto my clothes. The door from the back seat had somehow come off its hinges. It broke into pieces, and a shard had flown through to the front and sliced off a piece of my scalp. The car was a mess.

The ambulance came for me and picked up the piece of my scalp to see if the doctors could sew it back on. When I got to the hospital, I was still in such shock, I didn't feel anything. It was only when the doctor started looking at my wound and touching it, that I screamed; they gave me medicine for the pain. The doctors were trying to decide how far the wound had gone into my head. They finally decided that the hair would not grow back and was too big a piece not to have any hair growing on my head in that spot. So they squeezed my scalp together as close as they could and sewed it, leaving me with a long narrow scar. I thank God for that decision rather than the alternative.

The police officer who had first arrived at the scene of the accident stopped by at the hospital. "You don't know how lucky you are. That piece of metal that skinned your scalp could have gone deeper and caused a lot more damage if you hadn't put your head and body down," he said. Of course,

I knew it wasn't luck. Even though I hadn't surrendered my life to Christ, God was protecting me. At that point in my life, I still didn't understand how satan wants to kill and destroy the people God loves.

They kept me in the hospital for close to a week. I returned to work with medical bills and still no money to pay them. The driver had been arrested and went to jail for a couple of days, pending his court date. The police wanted my friend and me to file a full report of what happened. The driver was trying to blame me. He said I had grabbed the wheel, which made him lose control of the car. Of course, our story was very different. He was convicted of drunk driving and lost his license. My parents suggested I sue the driver's insurance company for medical bills and loss of work, and the lawyer insisted I sue for emotional trauma as well. It had been hard for me to sleep, and I began to hate being a passenger in a car. This didn't bode well for my ride to work.

So, my lawyer and I settled with the insurance company to pay my medical bills, loss of job, his fee and give me $10,000 for emotional damage. At that point, I was homesick. I missed my family and friends back home and it seemed that since I came to Chicago, there was nothing there for me but trouble. My father suggested buying a car with the money and coming back home. I had told them not to come to Chicago while I was in the hospital. I knew Dad couldn't leave the farm even for a week with no one to care for the animals and crops, even though they would have come if I asked them to. So, I sent my father $7000 to buy this beautiful black and white 1957 Chevy Convertible that he had sent me a picture of. Dad knew cars well, so I trusted his judgment. I should have sent him all the money.

My friend from Wisconsin drove me to the bus station. While we were sitting in the bus depot restaurant, I decided to go to the restroom. I had put the remaining $3,000 cash in a small wallet inside my purse and left out a little for my trip home. My intention was to keep the large amount of cash separate, so I wouldn't have to take it out of my purse. I had taken my lipstick and comb out of my purse to use in the bathroom. To this day, I don't remember how the rest happened. I must have taken the wallet out to get my comb. There was no one else in the restroom. I walked out, somehow leaving my small wallet sitting on the bathroom counter. I went straight back to my seat and sat there for a couple of minutes while we waited for the check. As I picked up the bill and began reaching for my money, I noticed my wallet was gone. Panicked, I ran to the bathroom. There was no one there, and I hadn't seen anyone go to the restroom. The wallet was nowhere to be found. I informed the manager, but there was nothing he could do.

I was sick to my stomach. It was a good thing I had $300 for food and my bus ticket home set aside. The ride home was terrifying. The bus driver drove so fast I kept reliving my accident again and again. I couldn't wait to get home.

CHAPTER 6

Could it be Love?

I loved my car. It was black with a white convertible top; even though it was three years old, it looked like it had just come off the assembly line. It was the envy of all my friends. If I hadn't lost all the rest of my money, I probably wouldn't have been in a hurry to find a job. But I needed money to drive my beautiful car, and my parents said I had to pay my own insurance. In those days, children were expected to either get a job to pay their way through college or get a job, period. Since neither of my parents had gone to college and they were comfortable with their life, they felt my brother and I should just get a job. Later they changed their minds about higher education when it came to my younger sister and paid for her to go to business school.

Getting Jobs

My brother was still partying and drinking. He couldn't keep a job. He was either late or wouldn't show up at all after a night of heavy drinking. He had already become an alcoholic. He had joined the National Guard as the Vietnam War went on, but he even messed up there. So, he asked to be transferred to regular military service, and that upset my parents. They did not want him sent to Vietnam. But through God's grace, he was sent to Germany instead. However, the Army was not going to put up with his addiction to drinking and now newly found drug use. He came home on leave for a week and did not make it back to Germany because of a drinking binge. My parents were notified that he was AWOL by his Sergeant, and the authorities were looking to arrest him.

David woke up with a terrible hangover after days of being in a stupor, and knew he was in deep trouble. He called me and asked what to do, so I went to pick him up and called my parents to let them know what happened. I told my brother to call his sergeant at the base and explain the truth. They had a good relationship, and when David wasn't drinking, he had a winsome personality and was well-liked by everyone he met. So that's what he did, and the sergeant told him to come back. He would have to be put in confinement for a few days, but since he hadn't intended to go AWOL, he would be let off with a slap on the wrist. The Vietnam War was starting to wind down, and he continued to stay in the army for another year, and then came home.

I realized I didn't have the proper education or much experience for any job. I could have applied for another office job, but I needed more money than that kind of job provided. It never occurred to me that you must work hard starting out to get better pay later. My parents had worked hard for everything they had, but we had been given everything as kids without any responsibility.

I had an entitlement mindset and expected everything would be easy, and so when I saw an ad in the newspaper for a waitress in a new city nightclub, I pounced on it. A friend told me I could make good tips in a place like that. Back in my Chicago days, I would have thought, "Oh, a nightclub, how glamorous and exciting!"

No one takes their mother to a job interview, but I did and to this day, I don't know why. But, to the club owner, a man twelve years older than me, having emigrated from Greece, this made me stand out to him as a good girl who had been sheltered. He started to tell me about the job and then pulled a skimpy uniform out of the desk drawer and explained that this was a real nightclub, and all the girls wore these outfits. Before he could say anymore, I said, "Oh, I can't wear that; my dad would be so mad!"

He seemed to hesitate, then said, "You won't have to wear it, I'm hiring you to do my office work."

Although the club was very large, there wasn't enough room for two people to work in his small office. He was very handsome, and I could tell right away he was interested in me. The nightclub was beautiful and glamorous. It fit into my movie star image, and I needed the job, so I agreed to do his office work. Later, I realized there wasn't any office work for me; he just wanted me around. It was boring with days spent sitting in his office with nothing to do. It wasn't long before he let his true intentions show.

There were lots of other women working there, and he was very business-like with them. Even when they would try and flirt with him, he just ignored it. He flirted with me, though, and didn't want me talking to other men. I thought he was a very exciting man, someone so self-assured, who seemed to know every important person in the city. But none of that drew me in. I was never interested in a man with money or power. I was brought up in the simple life, and I was used to getting material things I wanted, so it never impressed me.

It was his interest in me and his good looks, his way of treating me special and his desire to protect me that began to win me over. Subconsciously, I was looking for someone who would do what my father had failed to do—protect me from any abuse like my mother's. I took his trying to keep me from other men and not wanting me to work as a waitress as loving protection. I didn't realize it wasn't about love: it was about control.

As we dated, he told me that he had grown up in Greece, and he and his brothers had immigrated to America when he was only seventeen. He also told me he had gotten along well with his father but not with his mother and felt that she was very hard on him. I didn't realize at the time that he had the same problem I did, and all his self-assuredness and need to control was to stop being hurt inside. However, as with many young women, I didn't see what was coming; I was too busy living a fairy tale life with my handsome prince. I should have realized after we dated for a while how controlling he could be.

On one of my weekends off, I decided to go to my aunt's cabin in Northern Michigan. There was a place up there called The Music Box, and I had gone every summer. It was an outdoor venue where all the high school and college students went to party and dance. It was one of my favorite spots in the summer months. So, I let him know I would ride up with my aunt and uncle to the lake and stay for the weekend. Right away, he was mad. "You're not going!" he said.

"What do you mean I'm not going?" I replied. With my strong, independent personality, I wasn't used to anyone telling me I couldn't do something.

"I said, you can't go," he repeated, "because I want you here!"

Mad, I said, "I'm going," and walked away. I think it shocked him since he was so used to getting his way with others.

I left for the lake the next morning but decided to drive the two-and-a-half hour stretch separately from my aunt. After I was there for about half a day, I began to feel bad about his hurt feelings. I also realized I was developing deep feelings for him. So, just before bedtime, I told my aunt I was going back home. She didn't want me to travel at night, but I left anyway—you know how indestructible young people think they are.

At the same time that night, he had gone to my parents' house to get my brother out of bed to ride with him up to the lake to get me since he didn't know where it was. Imagine him and my brother on their way up north while I was on my way back. At the time, I thought it was funny and was just a sign he really loved me. But it was pure, simple control, because neither of us knew the meaning of love.

Marriage

We could have learned real love if we had surrendered our lives to God. Instead, we went the way of many relationships without God. We married and had two wonderful daughters. At first, he wasn't verbally abusive, just controlling. I began to treat him like a God and tried to please him in every way I could, but this behavior seemed to make him angry. He became more and more verbally and physically abusive. I told him to stop, or I would leave him and take the children. So, he stopped the physical abuse; that was the one thing I was never going to allow to happen to my children or me. He was good to the children though. He loved and cared for them, sometimes like a mother. We adored our girls. We were married for seven years.

Up to then, there had been no divorce in my family. My mother and father were married for over fifty-five years and left this world married to only each other. I should not have put up with the lack of respect he showed me, but I continued to try and please him. I had married for keeps, just like my parents. But, as fate would have it, that was taken out of my hands.

Both of us had experiences with God in the past. I tried to talk to him once about my feelings toward God. He said I sounded like his grandmother, so I surmised she was a believer. He also mentioned that God had wanted him to be a priest in the Greek Orthodox church, but he wanted to make money and be successful first, and then he would acknowledge God's call. That was the last time in our marriage we talked about God. We both had journeyed down the wrong road instead of the one God had set out for us.

I stayed home with the children, and he continued to run the nightclub and purchased another restaurant down the road. He stayed out very late one night, and at first, I thought it was because the nightclub didn't close until 2 a.m. and sometimes the club bar owners would meet for coffee after they closed. I was not a jealous person, so I didn't believe he would cheat. But soon after my second child was born, I learned to mistrust men.

I don't remember exactly how I found out but I was friends with the restaurant chef, and I believe she was the one who told me he was seeing someone. I confronted him about it, and he didn't lie. I told him if he continued, I would take the children and leave. He told me he was sorry and that it wouldn't happen again. "I don't want you to leave," he said. A little while later, I found out he was still seeing her; again, he again begged me not to leave. He told me that he had called it off with her. He was the first man I'd ever loved, and we both loved our two children. I so wanted to believe him. But, really, he was just playing her like he was playing me. He was caught in a web of his own lies, and he didn't have the courage to tell the truth and decide to do what was right. This went on for quite a while. I knew I couldn't live with him cheating on me, so I told him I wanted a divorce.

He begged me not to divorce him and vowed to find a way to get out of the arrangement with her. "Every time I talk to her about breaking up with her, she cries," he said. He thought I was stronger than her and could handle it because I would never cry in front of him. I cried plenty, but only when he and the kids couldn't see me. By then I weighed ninety-five pounds, and my bones showed. I started having nightmares with satan telling me I was unlovable and stupid, just as my mother and husband had. In the nightmares, satan would always say, "You should kill yourself."

One night after my husband had moved out, I woke up in the middle of the night from a nightmare that scared me to death. In the dream, we had a big picture window in front of our house. I was sleeping on the couch facing the window, and one night I got up and looked out the window at night. The girl he was living with now was driving by, and her face was ugly and contorted. She looked right at me, laughing hysterically. After I woke up, I didn't want to go back to sleep. I was still not a believer and didn't realize these were demons and yet another attempt by satan to destroy me. He wanted to prevent me from becoming a Christian and have the power and authority of the name of Jesus Christ over him.

The divorce went through, even though he continued to ask me not to do it. This affair could go on forever, and he still had an anger issue when he couldn't get his way. As much as he loved his children, he couldn't control his ugly words even when the children were present. I knew it was bad for the children to be exposed to their dad when he was like that. Also, the stress was causing me health problems. Not only was I not eating, I wasn't getting sleep either.

The children and I continued to live in our house. I had the children full time except for weekends and some holidays. He eventually married his girlfriend, and they had two children. His desire was to see that all his children loved each other, so he worked very hard to instill that in them. They were all family.

CHAPTER 7

Going No Where

Instead of turning to God, I was still looking for someone who would treat me right and be my protector. But I had heard so many stories about bad second marriages where children were involved, I had decided that I would marry a man that would to be good to me and my children. My children came first, even before a husband. I made up my mind, I would be a good wife to whomever I married, and that was all that I needed. What a fool I was to think I had the wisdom to pick the right man for my children and me! Also that any man could fill the place in my heart that only God could!

Without a relationship with God, I could not be the wife any man needed either. I stayed single for about a year, while my ex-husband continued to interfere and control my life. But I didn't go out to clubs anymore; I really didn't have the desire to, and now that I had children, I didn't think it was the right thing to do. But my girlfriend kept saying, "I can't believe your ex-husband is living with a woman, and you just sit at home. This is what he wants; that's why he thinks he can have his cake and eat it too," she said.

Feeling lonely and dejected, I finally gave in to my friend's invitation to go to the nightclub. I had not danced since I married my husband. I told myself I'd go just this once, just to dance, but I didn't want any relationship. I even got my cousin to join us.

We had a good time dancing. None of us girls drank alcohol, so we sat there drinking coke and dancing with whoever asked us. The men showed us a lot of attention. Night club attendance was an acceptable way to meet the opposite sex during this time, and dancing was also a good way to meet someone.

As we left the club and got into the car, my cousin who was driving noticed a car behind us as we began to pull out. "That looks like your ex-husband's car behind us." We had just pulled up to enter the main highway out of the club parking lot. This was a bustling highway, but thank God it was late at night, so there was less traffic. He rammed the back of our car, which sent us shooting out into the highway. Only God's protection kept us from hitting another vehicle. Later in life, all three of us girls would surrender our lives to God and become Christians. But at the time my cousin and girlfriend were scared, and I was mad.

When I got into the house, my phone started ringing. It was him. He said, his friend who owned that club had called him. "I don't want the mother of my children going to some club like street women" (I won't use the word he used). I knew He still felt he owned me and did not want his friends to see me out. Also, when it came to morals, they only applied to women, not men. I agreed that it wasn't appropriate for me, not because of him but my own convictions. I didn't want to be the kind of mother hanging out at bars.

I kept thinking about what my ex had said about not wanting the mother of his children going to clubs like some street woman. Who did he think he was? It made me so mad; what a hypocrite! He committed adultery, and that was alright for a father to do, and he even moved in with her before they were married. He didn't think that would hurt his children. Well, that kind of reasoning is dangerous because it brings on a spirit of retribution. Two wrongs don't make a right.

No, going to clubs was not the answer, but I was sick of him trying to control me. So, I decided that I would go again. I told my girlfriend I had warned him, "If you ever do that again, I will call the police!"

Would this Marriage Work?

We had a great time dancing and, yes, we were asked out. But we turned the men down. One man who was shy and not a big talker, who was a great dancer, kept asking me to dance, and we danced very well together. Many dancers would stop and watch us. He came to my table in between music breaks. I did most of the talking since he was so shy. I liked that about him; it reminded me of my father. He seemed like a nice guy. He was an ordinary looking guy, and he didn't use foul language. I wouldn't give a guy the time of day who did. And the way he approached me about asking for my phone number was not too pushy. He just said, "I really would like to talk to you again. Would you mind giving me your phone number?"

I thought, "What's the harm in talking to him? He's not asking me for a date."

He called me a few days later and we talked. He told me he was single and had never been married. He said he had enlisted in the navy right after high school and traveled the world. He had only been home a year, lived with his parents and had a job with the airlines. I told him about my life. He said it sounded like the same thing that happened to his mother when his dad had left her.

The one thing that attracted me to him was he seemed kind and a gentleman, though very shy, not like a man that would try to control anything. So, I agreed to meet him, but on condition he did not come when my children were home because I didn't want to confuse them by bringing men around. He said he respected me for that; it was agreeable with him. So, when we dated, I would take my children to my mother to babysit, and then he would pick me up at my house. He started calling me every day, and I enjoyed talking to him.

His childhood had been troubled. His dad left when he was young, and his new stepfather was not a good role model. Ted seemed to rebel against his mother and had a minimal relationship with his father and stepfather. Whereas I became angry and didn't hold my feelings back, Ted kept all his feelings inside. I later found out he really wasn't honest with me about how he felt about his life. But one thing we both had in common was that we loved to dance. But you had to be an extrovert to continue a conversation with him because he was so quiet when the dance was over. And of course I was one.

But he did open up to me some because I asked him questions. I didn't like his family when I dated him. His stepfather was very vulgar. That was something I hadn't grown up with. My father was a modest man and wouldn't even take his shirt off in front of his children. I'd never heard a vulgar word from my mother and father. How strange I thought it was! Ted was such a gentleman and never was vulgar or used foul language. He was so different from his family. I did like his two younger sisters, who seemed more like their brother. After we dated for a while, I really liked him and decided that was all I needed to feel in marriage.

Again, this was not wisdom. I didn't realize how hurt I was from my first marriage. At that time, I decided to let him be around my children and extended family. I had talked to him about how much their dad and I loved and valued our children. Because he had been through having a stepfather, I thought he would understand my need to have a good stepfather to my children. And it wouldn't be like how he grew up; instead, my children had a good father who would be very active in their lives, and he just needed to be a good role model and friend to them. He also knew how I felt about a man being faithful. I brought him to a family gathering at my parent's home, and they liked him.

My children were still young, and I should have seen some of the signs then about his relationship with them. He was nice to them but didn't know how to talk or play with young children. At the time, I thought that was okay: he'd get more relaxed with them later. Without God, I couldn't see the warning signs. I had chosen the men I wanted to marry twice, instead of letting God choose. I didn't have any relationship with God at the time and didn't even think about asking God about dating or marriage. That wasn't how the world taught me to find a mate. So, we married, and I continued down the wide road to destruction and sorrow.

CHAPTER 8

Spiritual Encounters

Before I tell you about our marriage, my younger sister, Shirley, had married her high school sweetheart. He was a Christian and had asked her to visit his church with him. They gave an altar call at church, and she went forward and gave her life to Christ. Her husband liked to ride his motorcycle up to Northern Michigan on the weekends. With its tall pines, white birch trees, and blue lakes, it's one of the most beautiful places in the summer.

The Accident

That weekend was no different as he and Shirley and another married couple left early on a Saturday morning. A few miles out of town, they had been riding their motorcycles side by side as they always did for safety. For some reason, Shirley's husband's friend, who was in Bible College studying for ministry, decided to pull ahead of my brother-in-law and sister. They drove on for about two blocks, and a drunk driver came through the stop sign on a side road and hit my brother-in-law's cycle. My sister was thrown from the cycle up against a pole.

My brother-in-law was not hurt. But the impact had mangled my Shirley's leg beneath the knee. She was in shock, but one of the first people at the scene said she just kept saying over and over, "God help me!"

We were all notified what had happened and that she was at the city hospital. What I remember about that was her pain. She was in intensive care. They were waiting to amputate her leg and we were all taking turns going in to see her. They had given her pain medication when she first arrived but had stopped it because the doctor was due any minute and they would have to sedate her in surgery.

My mother had just been in to see her, and she said Shirley was in unbearable pain and was begging the doctors to give her something. They said they were so sorry, but they couldn't. On top of that the doctor was held up in his own surgery due to complications. When Mother came out, she asked who wanted to go in next. No one spoke up, including my dad or her husband. I knew they couldn't bear to see her in so much pain, so I went back in. She had bitten through her lip so hard it was bleeding, and was in too much pain to talk. So, I waited a few minutes, even though it was so hard to watch.

I walked back out and asked if someone else would go in, but everyone was

hesitant. I couldn't leave her alone. It wasn't because my family wasn't compassionate. Shirley was the baby of the family, but this was to be an arranged moment for me, one that was to be one of the keys in my journey to seeking God.

As I walked back into the room, what I saw was amazing. She was lying there looking peaceful and had a glow about her, almost angelic.

"What happened to you? I thought they were not going to give you any more pain meds before surgery," I asked.

"They didn't," she said. "I asked Jesus to take the pain away from my leg and He did." She was to tell me later that, when she asked Him, the pain left instantly. This was the first time I had heard about anything like this since I had read about the miracles Jesus did in the Bible. I was so shocked that I didn't know what to say, and turned around and walked out.

She had surgery. They tried to save her leg above the knee, so she could be fitted with an artificial leg and have more strength to walk with it, but gangrene soon set in, and the doctors had to amputate part of her upper leg as well. While we were waiting to see if the leg circulation would start and they could save it, people came from my sister's church including the Pastor. No one asked to pray with my family, or prayed while they were there. Everyone just kept saying what a tragedy to happen to such a nice girl. I didn't realize Jesus was still doing miracles through His spirit on the earth, but I thought it was strange no one asked to pray with us.

Shirley was in the hospital for quite a few days after the surgery. One of the days I went to visit her, I asked her if she was scared about her future. Again, this was to be a Jesus moment for me, and I thank God for my sister's boldness at that time. She said that she had asked God, "What is my husband going to do?" She wondered if he would leave her since they were just married. What about having children— how was she to take care of them?

"I was starting to feel sorry for myself and scared about my future," she told me. "While I was thinking and talking to God, the maintenance worker came into my room, and said they had been renovating the hospital, and were replacing all the pictures in the room. Now this was a city hospital and, as far as anyone knew, there were to be no religious pictures. But this worker proceeded to put a picture of Christ carrying His cross up a hill, right on the wall at the foot of my bed. As I looked at it, God spoke to my heart. He said, 'And you think you have suffered!'"

She thought, "Jesus, if You could go through that for me, then I will be able to take a future with one leg. I know You have gone before me and will be with me." Again, I was amazed. It seemed the God my sister was talking to was the same one the Bible talked about.

So many times, the Spirit of God tries to reach us through different circumstances, but we still think we have it altogether and can handle everything by ourselves. Well, it was not long after marrying my second husband that I soon realized I had made a mistake. It wasn't really anything he did; I just didn't have the feelings a woman should have for her husband. But by that time I was pregnant. I believed I carried a lot of hurt and rejection and wasn't ready for another marriage. He also carried insecurities that made it impossible for him to share his feelings and to trust anyone. Also, he carried some dark sins that he hid from everyone, including me.

We settled into a fairly "normal" life. My father and mother gave us some land next to them to build a house. My husband made a pretty good salary in the airlines, and my ex-husband made sure our two girls had everything they needed. Soon my youngest daughter was born. Both her dad and I were thrilled. I will never forget the look on his face the moment he looked at his newborn daughter in my arms, and she opened her beautiful big brown eyes and looked at him. She had his heart from that moment on.

After my first divorce, I had thought in my heart "God, if I just have a good and faithful husband I will be happy. I just want someone who will love me and love my kids." And God gave me what I asked for. I had a nice new home, lived next to my parents, who were loving grandparents, had an ex-husband who had not abandoned his children, a new husband that said he loved me, and adored his new daughter. What more could a young woman want?

Yet I felt empty and alone. After a while I dreaded my husband coming home. I felt trapped but I had three children who meant the world to me, and I knew the worst thing I could do would be to leave him. So, I poured myself into being a good wife without the feelings for it. I also poured all my real affection onto my children, but I still couldn't shake the emptiness. I knew something was missing and it was more than a lack of feeling for my husband. I still wanted to blame my mother and my ex-husband for my problems. I wasn't ready to admit there might be something wrong with me. After all, hadn't I tried to please people—and look where it had got me? Wasn't I the victim?

Filling the Emptiness

I tried to fill the nagging emptiness in my life by taking a sculpture class at the local college, because I loved to create and paint. Sculpture seemed like something I would enjoy. At the time, the art teacher was a renowned artist in her own right. I set up a little room in my basement to sculpt. It was so relaxing—almost like taking a drug that calms you (which, thankfully, I never did). Whenever the kids went to bed, I would go down to my studio and work on a project. When my husband came home from work after dinner, he didn't want to talk, but would rather watch TV until he went to bed.

The sculpting studio became a retreat for me. We were growing more apart. At the same time, the thought kept coming to me about how I felt as a teenager when my two grandmothers died, and I didn't have anyone to talk to. I remember asking God to remind me how I felt, and when I was older, I could help someone. Of course, He did remind me as it was part of His plan for my life.

I read an article in our city newspaper about Social Services being overwhelmed with teenagers who were getting into trouble with drugs. It was the early 70s, the time of the hippie movement—the free love revolution, no absolute truth or God, just LSD and heroin. The article said that no one wanted to foster teenagers in their homes. After reading the article, I began to feel so burdened for these kids that I asked my husband if we could become foster parents. He thought I had enough on my hands with my family, but he agreed that it was okay. He had such a hard time being a parent that he was happy to let me take the responsibility of raising the children.

We began the process of taking a night course of ten weeks to become foster parents. Like many new foster parents, I thought that all I had to do was love these kids, be good to them, give them someone to talk to, and it would change the direction of their life. I had made the biggest mistake that most foster parents make when thinking about helping a child. These children hurt so bad that they don't know how to trust real love. And the sad thing was, I felt the same way too.

It takes years for their hearts to heal and sometimes they won't accept their healing. Quite a few foster parents give up and ask that the children be removed from their home. This only proves to the child that no one can love them and it's the worst thing a foster parent can do. The child leaves and is put into the vicious cycle of going from one foster home to another. It is funny that I thought at the time I could help anyone when I felt so empty and unhappy. But God had a plan.

Before our classes were done, a couple of friends came to my house and wanted to talk to me about God. One friend had just turned her life over to Jesus and was very excited. I knew that she and her husband were having trouble in their marriage. She thought her husband was cheating on her but couldn't prove it. She said she was going to put her husband and marriage in God's hands; no matter what her husband decided to do, she was going to walk with God. There was a peace about her that I knew was real.

But then they began to question me about my beliefs. I felt they were implying I didn't believe in God. Whenever I thought someone was criticizing me, I became defensive. Of course, they weren't really criticizing me, they were concerned for me and wanted to share what happened to them. I asked them to leave. "I don't want to talk to you about this."

They told me later that when they got into the car they said, "Were we wrong? Maybe the Holy Spirit didn't tell us to come here at this time."

Many Christians believe that if someone rejects their message they were not sent by God. Christians must know that the person is not rejecting them but rejecting God. Like many people seeking God, God was trying to get me to see the truth, but satan was working hard to stop me.

After they left, I felt bad for treating them that way, but on the other hand, I thought, "Who do they think they are, thinking they are better than me?" As I was washing the dishes from our lunch, I thought about what they had said. I said to God simply, "I just want to know You." At that moment, I began to feel a dark and a chilling presence standing beside me. My body began to shake. This evil presence spoke to me these words: "I want you to give yourself to me and serve me."

I knew it wasn't God. It reminded me of the terror dreams I had when I discovered my first husband was cheating on me. I turned to this dark presence beside me and said, "Even if I go to hell, I will never serve you." I felt something rise in me that's hard to explain, "I love God," I said.

When I look back, it was God again intervening in my life and protecting me from satan. But at the time, I didn't have the kind of relationship and knowledge of God to protect myself. As soon as I said, "I love God," the dark presence left. There are many Christians that think God doesn't answer the prayers of people who haven't accepted Jesus as the Savior of their sins; but the truth is God answers the prayers of the one who is seeking Him in order to bring them to His Son.

My husband and I finished our foster care classes. Social Services were so desperate for foster parents for teenagers, they asked us immediately if we would take a teen in. We said yes, but it would have to be a girl. With our three girls, we didn't think it would be a good idea to have boys around our girls.

Healed of Addiction

About the same time, I was waking up every morning with a raging cough. I had smoked cigarettes for a few years, since my first job in Chicago. The girls in my office said it helped them lose weight. I thought I needed to lose a few pounds, so not only did I start, but I became so addicted that I was up to three packs a day and would rather smoke than eat. I became so addicted that if I was out of cigarettes late at night, I would go to the local 24-hour gas station and buy them. I became alarmed when I would cough so much but didn't seem to have a cold.

I decided to go see a doctor. After he ran all the tests, he told me I had some black spots on my lungs. If I didn't stop smoking, my children would not have a mother in five years. That got my attention. The last thing I wanted was to leave my children for someone else to raise. I went home and cried. "How am I going to stop?" I thought. I had tried everything before.

I became afraid I was going to die. I had always believed as a child that if God was real, there wasn't anything He couldn't do. So, one night when everyone was in bed, I sat down at my kitchen table and looked up. "God, if You're real, then can You help me? I can't stop smoking. God, I've tried so hard to stop and I don't want to leave my children." I didn't really care about my unhappy marriage, but I cared about the kind of life my children would have. God knew that He could use my love for my children to let me have another miraculous God moment. This time, I would learn just how powerful He is.

Right after that prayer, I heard Him in my mind call me by name, "Dolores, throw away your cigarettes." I only had half a pack to get me through until the bedtime, and I thought I couldn't survive without them and coffee in the morning.

So, I said to Him, "I've done that before and ended up going and buying more."

"This time, it will be different," He said.

I don't know why, but I knew it would be. So, I crushed my cigarettes and threw them away. About an hour later, I wanted a cigarette.

He spoke to me again, "You went for one hour. You can go another hour."

"I've gone through that train of thought before and it didn't work."

Again, He said to me, "It will be different this time."

For some reason, even without really knowing God, I believed Him and thought "Okay." As soon as I agreed with God, the desire for a cigarette left me. This debate went on for seven days. After that, I was no longer addicted to cigarettes. I thought, "God is real, and He cares about me and my family."

Later, I was to hear and see God delivering others of addiction to alcohol, drugs, and cigarettes instantly. I would think, "Why did I have to go seven days?" But God spoke to my heart that I had such a strong addiction that, if it was made easy for me, I would go back to smoking again. He deals with each one of us according to our personalities since He has made each one of His children unique. He knew me better than I knew myself. I loved smoking too much, but He knew I loved my children more.

CHAPTER 9

The Coffee House

Right after I was delivered from my cigarette addiction, a foster teen that was addicted to drugs came into my life. They asked if I would go to the hospital to see her, as she had overdosed. Her parents, who were from an upper middle-class background, didn't know how to handle her rebellion anymore. At first, I thought, "What am I going to say to her?" Then the thought came to me, "Just ask her questions and talk to her and see how she feels. Ask her what she is going through in her life."

Ann

When I walked into the hospital room, there was a very pretty girl with long dark brown hair. She looked so young even though she was 16, and even though she was on drugs, she looked so innocent. I introduced myself and said that this was my first time being a foster mother. I told her a little about my family and why I wanted to be a foster parent. Then I asked her if she wanted to share with me why she ended up in the hospital.

She began to tell me about a twenty-year-old boy she was in love with. She would meet him secretly without her parents' permission. They didn't like him because they thought he was too old for her and they suspected he had introduced her to drugs— which he had. She said she loved this guy and wasn't giving him up.

I asked, "Why don't you want to live in a foster home?"

She said, "I've been in one. I don't like it."

I told her that Social Services would not give her a choice. "If you won't stay in a foster home, they will send you to a group home." I asked her if she would try staying with us. If she didn't like it, it would be okay and she could go to the group home, but either way they wouldn't let her see this boy while she was underage and under social service's supervision. I said I would come back the next day for her answer.

In the meantime, my friends were saying, "How can you bring these kids who are on drugs into your home with your children? They will be a bad influence on them." But God was to prove them wrong over the years. What my children learned from these teens was these were nice kids who got in with the wrong friends, made wrong choices, and a lot of times were looking for a love they didn't find at home. My children didn't want to make choices that led them in a direction that brought so much trouble to their lives.

Whenever you follow God's leading to do what He wants you to do, He will bless you and your family. The next day when I went back, she said, "Hi! I'm going home with you!" On the way home she told me, "When you walked into my room, you didn't look like my idea of a foster mother. You looked so young (I had just turned thirty) and you dress like me!" What she meant was I wore jeans and kept my hair straight and long. Really, as it turned out, God had brought a replica of myself at her age. She was the only girl in her family, and her mother and she clashed about everything. Her mother was a socialite and dressed her little girl to impress her friends. She would take her to her social club to show her off.

At the age of twelve her sweet little girl wanted to make some decisions on her own about what she wore. This again was the time of bell bottom jeans—no pretty dresses— but her mother wanted her to stay a little girl forever. She couldn't tell her mother how she felt; she just became angry and decided she would do what she wanted, whether her mother liked it or not. Her father was a lot like mine—gentle, kind, but quiet, and didn't want confrontations with her mother. She loved both parents but got along with her father better. After a couple of years of altercation with her mother, she started hanging around with friends that also had problems with parents. Then she met this twenty-year-old guy that showed her the kind of attention she was not getting at home. He liked her just as she was and listened to her.

I enrolled her in high school as we lived in a different town than she had come from. This is one of the things that is very hard on foster children. A lot of the children are in foster homes because of abusive parents through no fault of their own. Then they must go through the fear of going to a new school, leaving their friends and family behind, and trying to adjust to a new family and friends. Kids can be so cruel to each other, especially kids that have their own circle of friends and don't want to let in anyone new. It can be a very lonely and troubling time, especially for a teen foster child. The first day she had to attend high school alone, I watched from the car as she walked up the steps. I wanted to go in there and protect her from every stare and slight she would feel from other kids. One thing that always bugged me was anyone being cruel to another person.

And I really liked this girl. I liked everything about her, and God knew I would. That's why He sent her to be my first teen to live with us. My husband treated her like he did me. He had a couple of words for her when he came home from work; then turned on the TV to watch the rest of the night, except while eating dinner. I accepted her as one of my own children and treated her no differently. She fit in with my young children and my youngest, who was only three years old, seemed to really take to her. She would teach my young daughter how to pronounce words. She achieved high grades in school, was very artistic and would do ink drawings that were very beautiful in their detail.

But no matter how we all got along, she was very depressed and wanted to see her boyfriend. I couldn't let her do that as Social Services would make her leave my home if they found out. Besides, I knew it would not be good for her to see him. I thought, "I need to take her to church; maybe that will help her." The next Sunday, we went to the Catholic church, but she really didn't want to go. As we sat in the pew and watched the priest go through his rituals, speaking in Latin, I thought, "How will this help her? It never helped me." So, after we left, we didn't go back. But God was on the hunt, and He wasn't going to give up until He caught me. I didn't give up trying to help Ann either, but nothing seemed to work.

The Light Room

One night, I was reading the Sunday paper and was drawn to a front-page picture of a girl playing the guitar and singing. There was something in her eyes—she was looking up—that was so peaceful, almost like she was lifted someplace out of this world. I knew she was experiencing something I had never felt. Underneath the picture was an article about a Christian coffee house ministry called "The Light Room." It said the lives of these young people were changing through this ministry. What struck me was that the look on the girl's face singing in the picture was the same look on my sister Shirley's face when God took her pain away in the hospital.

"This is what Ann needs," I thought. The article went on to talk about a Friday night session where different groups played music and gave testimonies. I didn't know what giving testimonies was all about, but every church I visited played music, so I asked Ann if she would like to go. "I really don't want to go," she replied. I did not want to force her to go. I thought I really needed to go first and see what it was like before I took her.

A couple of days later I drove to the coffee house. The building was right in the heart of the city. I walked into a large room with tables and chairs set throughout. There was a coffee urn, and paper cups set out on a table, with a sign saying, "Free Coffee." A few young adults were sitting around talking and drinking coffee, and there were open bibles sitting on the tables. Most of the people there were under the age of thirty, except for a lady in her sixties, who was a visiting missionary from Nigeria. She wore a long skirt, which wasn't typical during the seventies. She said even though women in Nigeria wore similar long skirts, the only reason she still wore one in the States was to cover up her legs scarred by insect bites in Nigeria that itched so much.

Most of the boys in the Light Room Café sported beards and had long hair, straight or permed in the afro style of that era. Rock and roll was popular music during this time and so were bell bottom jeans.

The young man who had greeted me at the door introduced himself, "Hi! I'm Brad, I lead the ministry here for Trinity Assembly of God which supports this ministry as one of their outreaches. Is this your first time here?"

Even though I didn't know anything about the Assembly of God denomination or outreaches, I introduced myself. I told him the reason for my visit was my foster teenager that I wanted to help. He didn't try to push his beliefs on me, which I liked, but said, "You are welcome to bring her to our Friday night ministry meeting. There will be other young people and music she will like."

"Thank you, I will try to come."

The missionary was still standing with us. I asked her a few questions about her life and work, and she began to share with me about the miracles God was doing in Nigeria through her and other Christian missionaries. She said she was visiting Trinity Assembly of God because they helped support her ministry and she had heard the wonderful things God was doing through The Light Room Coffee House ministry and wanted to see it for herself. The miracles God was doing in Nigeria amazed me: people were being healed and even raised from the dead. She said these were documented by the many different missionaries from different countries working in Nigeria and other countries.

I thought "Wow! Jesus is still doing miracles on the earth, just like He did when He walked the earth!" Our generation in America think miracles are impossible and some Christians and denominations think God no longer does miracles. Our city newspaper, for example, carried a headline "God is dead!"

I couldn't explain it then, but I knew this was a humble woman who loved God and wanted all people to know and love Him. It reminded me of the Catholic nuns that I had admired for their dedication to God. I went home so excited I'd finally found something that would help Ann and she would be happy to be a part of; but when I asked her about going on Friday night, she said she didn't want to. I couldn't change her mind. I was so disappointed.

Denise and Me

At the same time, I had been trying to help my sister-in-law, Denise. She had been married to my brother for a while. I knew my brother was really messed up; he had come home from the Army still taking drugs and drinking. Denise was a beautiful woman. She had first married at fifteen, so by the time she was in her early twenties, she was divorced and had three children. Into her life walks my brother and they fall head over heels in love with each other.

Like me, without God in our life, we had no wisdom, so we couldn't value ourselves as God did. Denise had grown up with alcoholism in her family and she hated it as much as I did; but of course, my brother was able to stay sober for a short while, long enough to win her heart. He was a very kind and gentle man when sober but, like a Jekyll and Hyde, he'd turn violent and hateful when drinking. All the unforgiveness he had stored up in his heart reared its ugly head.

Denise was more like a sister than a friend, so our children spent a lot of time together and we grew to love each other's children. She had added another baby boy to her family, and she kept telling me how she felt at times like she was losing her mind with all the children to take care of. She adored her children. They meant everything to her, but all the responsibility of my brother going to the bar after work, spending his paycheck and not knowing in what condition he would come home was too much for her.

I noticed when I visited at different times, she would let the kids stay out in the backyard to play for long hours. They loved playing outside and were not complaining, but one time I asked her about the length of time they were outside, and she said, "I can't take all the noise in the house." This particular Thursday, I decided I would go by and visit her, and see how she was doing. On the way there the thought came to me about stopping at the Christian bookstore and buying her a bible, I had no idea why I thought about the Bible—I didn't even know if she already had one. When I got to her house she was so upset. "I've made an appointment with a counselor. I just can't take it anymore; I don't know what to do—I feel so trapped, like there's no way out," she said.

I gave her the bible and told her what happened when I went to the coffee house, also what the lady missionary had shared with me. "Denise, you don't need to go to a counselor; you need to go to the coffee house with me Friday night."

I was surprised I said that because I hadn't planned to go after Ann wouldn't, but somehow, I knew what Denise would find there was what she needed. What was funny, because of pride, I was not admitting to what I needed in my life also.

She looked at me like she was thinking about something. Then she said, "You know what? I'm going to cancel my appointment and go with you tomorrow night."

That decision would change the course of both our entire lives and start us on a life of joy. The next day was Friday, and I couldn't wait. "I'll pick you up at seven as it starts at eight," I said. I was so excited, I could hardly sleep that night and the day seemed to drag on as I couldn't wait for evening to come. I asked my mother if all the kids could stay with her and have dinner with her. She loved her grandkids, and she also liked my foster daughter. I picked up Denise and we talked all the way there. She shared how my brother acted when he was drunk and she talked about her money problems.

Even though my husband didn't drink, I couldn't get him to talk about anything and I had found pornographic magazines he had hidden. I was really mad about the magazines; I didn't want my children or foster teen exposed to anything like that. I also told her, "He spends a lot of time on the phone with friends at work betting on football games."

The coffee house was full when we got there. A band was on the stage getting ready to play. We walked over, got a couple coffees and tried to find a place in the back to sit. People were still coming in and we had to sit on the floor as all the chairs had filled up.

The young man that I had met when I first visited stood on the stage and greeted everyone. He asked everyone to join him in prayer, then introduced the band. When they started to play, I thought they were playing rock and roll; the music was so loud I could hardly hear the singer. Like many other people who didn't know who God was, because of my past experience, I thought you had to be quiet in church. God is holy, I thought and He wouldn't like some kinds of music—certainly not this loud! During the years I was growing up, the only kind of music you would hear in the denominations I visited was a piano or organ playing as a choir sang, and the congregation sang along with hymn books. I didn't realize, like so many people out of ignorance of God's word, I was trying to put God in a box and limit Him, thinking He can only do what human beings are capable of, and what we judge as good or bad.

As I sat there, I got more and more irritated, just as I had when my friends came to witness to me. "You need to get out of here!" I said to myself. I was about to get up and tell Denise we had to leave, when a voice spoke to my mind, and like it had so many times in my life, counteracted my thinking.

"Listen to the words they are singing. This is something you have looked for all your life," the voice said. I recognized this voice as the same voice that told me I would not die in the car accident when I was young. Yes, this was God speaking to me again. So I began to tune in to what they were singing—and then I heard them. They were singing about how wonderful God is and how much He loves us.

When they were through playing, a young man went to the stage and introduced himself and began to share a story about how Jesus intervened in his life.

"When I started college, I had my life all planned out: go to college, get a good paying job and retire at fifty years old." Then one day as a junior in college, he sat in class listening to a professor talk about all the damage humans were doing to the planet and how the massive population growth would cause so many disasters on the earth. The air, water, and food supply would be affected, and people would die by the millions from disasters and starvation in these students' lifetimes. The young man then thought, "This is crazy! Why am I going to college if there is no future? Why not go and have a good time?"

So, he left for the beach in Florida, where he partied every day, and was having a good time until one party got out of hand, and the police showed up. They arrested them for public drunkenness, some underage drinking, and for resisting arrest. As he sat in jail, he had time to reflect on his life, "I have really messed up, given up my education and now have an arrest record." He had never thought much about God before, and really didn't think he needed Him. They were going to be in that jail until their court date—unless someone bailed them out. He did not want his parents to know, yet he felt there was no one he could call on to help him. So he cried out to God, "If You get me out of this jail cell, and somehow I don't end up with a record, I will serve You the rest of my life."

The next day a policeman came to his cell and called out his name, "You're free to go."

"Why are you letting me go?"

"Because we know you didn't take part in the disturbance or resist arrest," he said.

"That was true," the young man thought, "but how did they know that?" The police had arrested everyone at the party; there also were others that had not been rowdy or resisted arrest, but they were still sitting in jail. He knew then that God had performed a miracle on his behalf. What was great was the policeman had said he would not have to go to court, and there would be no record. He at once thought, "I am heading back to my hometown and to college. God has set me free, and I want to make something of my life."

When he went back to college, he stopped drinking. But it wasn't long afterwards that he was back; he had put his promise to Jesus on the back burner. A couple of months later, as he was driving down the expressway not thinking about anything, a voice spoke to him out of the blue, "What about Me? Have you forgotten your promise?"

"The next thing that happened was hard for me to get my head around," he told us. "I had never had an experience like this before. But, as the voice spoke to me, I had a vision of Jesus Christ standing in front of my car filling the whole windshield. The thought came to me, "I am driving this car but all I can see is Jesus in my windshield? This is crazy!" God had stopped time for me. I confessed, "Jesus I am so sorry, I want to follow You; You can have my life; do whatever You like with it."

This young man would keep his promise this time. After finishing his education, and working in the coffee house ministry, he would go on to serve God. After he was through sharing his story, he asked, "If anyone wants to know this God that stepped into my life, please stand up and go into the prayer room, and others will go and pray with you."

I was amazed by his story and believed it. I thought I already knew God (what pride!) but the plain truth was I didn't want to get up in front of anyone, like it was shameful to admit I needed anything. I watched in amazement as my sister-in-law got up and went back to the prayer room. "Oh my gosh! She is going back there!"

It was over. Some were standing around talking, while my sister-in-law was still in the prayer room. She finally came out.

"What happened?" I asked.

"I prayed and gave my life to Jesus," she replied.

On the way home we talked about the story that guy had told. We were both excited about what God had done in his life. I noticed a glow in Denise's eyes, no more the frowning and sadness that I'd seen lately.

The next week I went over to her house, talked with her and watched her behavior toward her children. The transformation was amazing. She no longer complained about my brother; she just wanted to talk about Jesus. I also noticed the patience she had with her children. She seemed so peaceful; yet her circumstances hadn't changed. The thought came to me that God is not only real, He can change someone's unhappy life to one of joy and peace. For the first time I admitted to myself that this was what I needed.

Taking that Step

I knew the Assembly of God church that had supported the coffee house ministry was about thirty minutes from my home. Many of the young adults that attended the coffee house went there. I couldn't wait till Sunday. There were about two hundred and fifty people already seated as the announcements were being made. As I sat down, the choir and song leader began to sing worship songs. They were songs I had never heard in the previous churches I had visited; they made you feel like you were in the presence of God. I noticed people raising their hands, closing their eyes, and singing with such passion to God. They didn't care who saw them, or what people might think about them; they were just expressing their love for God and He was loving them back. I started to feel so bad about how my life had gone.

They had a wonderful Senior Pastor, an old man of God, who had such a loving spirit. I found out later his name was Pastor Snook; he usually spoke on Sunday mornings, while Assistant Pastor Lobbs spoke in the evening service. I also learned that this Senior Pastor was led by the Holy Spirit, and even if Pastor Snook had a sermon prepared, if the Holy Spirit directed to have Pastor Lobbs speak that morning instead, they would follow it.

So, this morning, Pastor Lobbs would be preaching God's word. The Holy Spirit always has a reason for the way he does things. This was how Pastor Lobbs' life and mine were to connect. As the Pastor began to open God's word to us and instruct us, it was as if he were telling the story of my life. As I became more and more burdened and weighed down by my own choices, I no longer felt sorry for myself for all the hurt and rejection I had felt. I thought no one made me make the choices I did so many times, even though I knew they were wrong. God had tried to reach me, but my pride made me turn away from Him, and made me try to solve my own problems.

While listening to Pastor Lobbs, I began to have a vision of my life from the time I was a little girl to the present. In this vision I could see every time God intervened in my life. I saw a little girl starting to build up anger and unforgiveness and not value herself as God valued her. It felt like bricks were one by one being laid on my back, bending me over with the burdens of life I had caused myself through rejecting God's love for me.

I knew Jesus died on the cross, but I didn't understand it was for me as an individual. The vision and the word of God the Pastor was preaching was opening my eyes to realize I had sinned by rejecting God and going my own way. By the time the Pastor gave an invitation to come forward and surrender our lives to Christ, I felt such a heavy load of sin on my back, I couldn't move even though I wanted to go to the altar.

"Jesus, I'm sorry; please take this monkey off my back" I cried. I don't know why I said it that way. I found out later some of the kids that were addicted to LSD, heroin and alcohol would say the same thing when they gave their life to God. I was just as bound as they were, only to unforgiveness and anger. As soon as I spoke, I felt the heaviness leave me and I ran up the aisle. I wasn't aware of anyone as I went. Even with so many people there, it was as if I was alone, and I knew Jesus was down there waiting for me. At the altar I fell to my knees. I don't remember anyone coming to me at the time, but I'm sure they did as people, and the Pastor would come and pray with a new believer.

I was so full of joy, all I could say was "I love You, Jesus," over and over. As I did, this picture began to form in my mind—not a vision this time. What I was seeing was faint, like looking through a mist. It was a picture of Jesus dying on the cross, but there was no one at the foot of His cross but me. He was in such pain, and His blood was falling like drops on my head. He didn't look down, but He spoke to me, "Are you willing to go down this road with Me? Are you willing to pay the price?"

"Oh, yes, Jesus. I want to serve You all of my life," I said. Of course, I had no idea how hard that road would be at times, nor did I understand all of what He meant. The only thing I knew was that I could no longer live without Jesus in my life. Just like other promises I made to Him, He not only would make sure I kept it, but would give me the ability through His Holy Spirit to do so.

CHAPTER 10

Experiencing the Presence of God

That was the most wonderful week for me as it was for my sister-in-law. I devoured the Bible, and the Word became alive to me. The thing I was curious about, and had never seen or heard before, was people speaking in strange languages, then someone giving an interpretation in English in the church service. Also, there were people giving what the Bible calls a "word of knowledge" or "word of wisdom" to the congregation, and the pastors and elders would pray for the sick. Those who were in bondage were delivered of demons. I had never been in a church like this before; it was like living in the New Testament early church times.

One of the guys from the coffee house who I asked what those people were doing told me, "Read the Book of Joel and 1 Corinthians, especially chapter 12, in the Bible." I went home and read the scriptures all week. I also went to a Christian bookstore to find a book to read. A book by a well known reporter caught my eye, a book on the baptism in the Holy Spirit. He said he was a Christian but did not believe in the supernatural gifts that were being manifested in certain churches. So, while investigating to prove these supernatural gifts were fake, he instead concluded that not only were they not fake, but were given to believers by the Holy Spirit.

He realized God was moving and pouring out His Spirit on his generation, and he wanted to be a part of it. This was the first time he had studied in depth what the Bible says about the Holy Spirit and His work in the Body of Christ. Now, instead of listening to others' interpretation of the word of God, he realized God had sent the Holy Spirit to empower the church, to build it up, to strengthen the Body of Christ and to make them witnesses until Jesus comes back for His Bride, the Church. The birth, death, and resurrection of Jesus would make it possible for the Holy Spirit that lived in Jesus while He walked the earth to now be poured out on His Church.

After reading the scriptures as well as this book, I decided I wanted all that God had for me. I knew the Holy Spirit had planted a seed of the new birth in me, and, because of what Jesus had done on the cross, I now was a child of my Father in Heaven. He had saved me, and brought my spirit to life in a right relationship with Him. Now I wanted to be filled to overflowing with His Spirit and make Him my Lord—not just my Savior but my Lord. I knew God needed to have complete control of me so He could use me in whatever way He saw fit. I wanted everyone to know my wonderful Savior. I saw in the Book of Acts before Jesus went back to His Father, how He told His disciples to wait for the Holy Spirit to come upon them and then they would receive power to be His witnesses throughout the earth.

I went to the Light Room Café every day that week, wanting to be around the excitement of what God was doing there. I took my youngest daughter with me; she would sit and play with the toys and children's books. There were always the few young ministry workers there, who had given their lives to Christ and been set free from bondages and addictions. After being set free, they were so in love with Jesus, they would share Him with people in the coffee house and on the streets. I wanted to be a part of this ministry too. But first I needed to learn more about God myself. Many times, some young adults would be sitting at the tables with others, drinking coffee, bibles open, reading and sharing with each other what the Holy Spirit was revealing to their hearts.

That first week I just soaked up all that everyone was sharing, asking questions and studying the word myself to see if what was being shared was truly God's word. When I got home, I couldn't wait to call my sister-in-law, and share with her what I had learned, and the miracles God was doing in this small coffee house. Not only would I share with her, I would share with my two oldest daughters, my teen foster daughter, my husband, and my mother and dad. I couldn't stop sharing the joy and excitement Jesus had given me. My children were young, and of course they believed me. My foster daughter didn't want to hurt my feelings, so she felt she had to listen to me. My husband was interested, but my mother didn't want to hear "all that God stuff." Strange that when I was so unhappy about my first marriage, she was very sympathetic, but now she didn't want to hear what had filled me with so much joy. I learned later in life that she had felt God wasn't there when she needed Him. We tend to blame God when things don't go right in our life and feel that He doesn't really care for us, which of course isn't true. It's our failure to seek God with all our heart, and not lean on our own understanding. This, of course, means trusting Him through the good and bad times. He knows what is ahead of us in the future: we don't. At the times I tried to share the Lord with my mother, I lacked discernment and wisdom, which the Holy Spirit gives us when we pray and ask for it. He is the only one who can open someone's heart to hear, and that comes when someone is earnestly seeking God. At that time my mother was not seeking God.

My dad was always like he was toward me; he smiled, listened and said, "That's good!"

One surprise for me was that I found out that my friend who had come to my home with her friend to witness to me—you know the one I threw out of my house—attended the same church. I called her and told her what happened to me. She was amazed. I also told her about my sister-in-law accepting the Lord in her heart. She was so excited to hear this. I know she had to be praising and thanking God after she hung up the phone because she had been obedient to come to my house that day. Before hanging up, I told her I would pick up my sister-in-law and we would see her in church on Sunday. All that week, I kept thinking about what the word of God said about being filled with the Holy Spirit. I was so in love with Jesus. I felt so free and clean, as if I had just been born into the world—no history behind me, only a glorious future. I had been born of God and, as a newborn looking into the face of my Father, I saw His love for me. Through the sacrifice of His Son, He had taken the heavy load of sin off my back and set me free.

Sunday was coming and I was so excited that I didn't sleep all night. I again asked my mother if she would watch my children. Ann, my foster daughter still did not want to come to church with me, so she stayed with my parents as well. I left early to pick up my sister-in-law. Again we talked all the way to church. But this time it was different; we didn't talk about what our husbands were doing wrong. Instead, we were sharing about what we were learning about God, and how much we were in love with Him. When we went into the church, I could at once feel the presence of the Holy Spirit. Like all services there, the Holy Spirit moved in the way He wanted to. As soon as we began to worship—and I don't mean programmed worship, I mean worship from the heart to the love of our life—God's presence met with each one of us individually.

As we continued to worship together, there was singing in languages other than English. It sounded like a choir of angels singing the same song, only in different languages. Then it would go from different languages to singing the same song in English. I felt like I was already in heaven. God was so close. As soon as the worship quieted down, the Holy Spirit began to speak through different people in the congregation. Some spoke in what the Bible describes as "unknown tongues;" these were called "unknown" because they were usually not languages anyone in the congregation spoke. There was also prophecy, words of wisdom and words of knowledge through the Holy Spirit among those gathered together. Just like scripture said, the church was coming together, all being used by the Spirit of God to edify and strengthen the Body of Christ. I knew what they were doing was of God, because the Holy Spirit had shown me through my study of God's word, that He gave gifts to people to not only build up the Body of Christ, but to equip them to preach the good news to the lost world.

When the Senior Pastor got up to speak, he spoke of our need not only to be saved and born again through Jesus' sacrifice, but to make Him Lord, asking Him to fill us with His Holy Spirit. What was so wonderful about the singing in the Spirit was that the words the Holy Spirit gave through the congregation were aligned with what the Pastor was teaching that morning. I realized later that this was how God confirmed what He wanted to tell His people that day.

His word says, "I will confirm My word with two or three witnesses." Much later in my walk with God, through the study of His word operating in the Body of Christ, the Holy Spirit began to show me that He doesn't use just the Pastor in the worship service. The Pastor is a ministry gift from Jesus, along with the ministry of Apostle, Prophet, Evangelist, and Teacher to equip the Body. Whenever The Holy Spirit uses a person, it is coming directly from God, not man's mind.

Rivers of Living Water

At the end of the service the Pastor gave an altar call, not just for salvation, but also for those who wanted to be filled with God's Spirit. As the Bible says, "Be filled with God's Spirit." I didn't know or understand all the scriptures yet, being a new babe in Christ, but I knew I wanted whatever Jesus had for me. So again I ran to the altar and right behind me was my sister-in-law. The altar was filling up, but I was oblivious to everyone around me, except a young man beside me. I was transfixed by him and what his eyes expressed, open and looking up full of joy. His arms were raised up to heaven, and he was speaking in an unknown language. There was perfect peace about him.

As I was watching him, the same missionary lady I had met at the coffee house ministry a few weeks ago came and stood beside me. "What do you want?" she asked.

When I answered her, I sounded like a little girl, "I have never done that before," referring to the young man beside me.

"You haven't? Well, honey, you will have rivers of living water running through you. Just tell Jesus, thank You," she said. So, I started to tell Jesus, thank You in English.

"Now, let the Holy Spirit say it through you," she said.

When I started to open my mouth to speak, my tongue suddenly felt heavy and I spoke two words that I knew in my spirit were, "Thank You," in Latin. I recognized the sound of it from the priests saying mass in Latin.

The next thing that happened—something I'm still in awe of today—was a loving Father talking to His child and giving her value. He said to me, "See you're not stupid, I gave you a new language in just a moment of time." He was speaking to a long time hurt: first, my mother's words making me feel like I couldn't do anything right, then, my first husband telling me in anger, "You're too stupid to learn the language of my country."

I know now after a few years of walking with the Lord, that God let me see into people's hearts, especially those that feel devalued and rejected. The Lord God, our Creator, is the only one who really esteems us with a pure heart. He proved that when He laid down His life for us while we were still sinners. I know how Mary Magdalene must have felt as she washed the feet of Jesus.

I now had what the New Testament disciples experienced in the Book of Acts when the Holy Spirit fell on them. My sister-in-law also received the infilling of God's Spirit that day. God was preparing me to be His witness, an ambassador of the gospel of Jesus Christ. As He spoke to my heart of His love for me, it was like a healing balm being applied to my soul.

I loved my parents and was afraid for them, as they were not believers. However, the Holy Spirit told me not to speak to my mother about God. Instead I was to pray for her to open her heart to Him, so that is what I began to do. I did share with my husband though, and I asked Jesus to give me love for him. It didn't happen overnight, but, little by little, I began to feel genuine affection and love for him. I could feel it flowing out of me to him from the Lord.

That next Sunday, I was to meet my friend Mary and sister-in-law Denise. We had planned to have lunch together after service. Again, the service was so exciting; I loved worshiping God with other believers. I knew He loved our praise and adoration to Him—after all, He is our loving Father. When I was worshiping Him, nothing else existed to me except God's passion for me and mine for Him. I'm not talking about passion in the way the world defines passion or love, because the world has no idea what those two words really mean.

I don't remember what the message was that day over fifty years ago, but I remember something I will never forget, something I have shared with very few people through the years, and only when the Holy Spirit prompted me. All the people from the coffee house went up to the altar at the end of the service every Sunday to pray for family and friends, and whomever God had put on their hearts.

Denise, Mary and I went up to the altar for the same reason; they were kneeling on either side of me. Mary's husband had left her for another woman. Mary had three children and was really hurting; Denise just wanted to worship, and so did I. After worshiping for a while, I began to feel an overwhelming presence of God. My eyes had been closed, but it felt like someone was standing in front of me. I thought it might be the Pastor as he usually walked back and forth praying for people. I opened my eyes.

As I did, it felt like my eyes were twirling—that's the only way I can explain the sensation. I knew God had done something with my eyes. Instinctively, the thought came to me, "My eyes will burn up if I am seeing Him with my natural sight. It's like looking directly at the noonday sun." I could only tell He was in the form of a man, with medium length hair just resting on His shoulders and He was dressed in a long flowing brilliant white robe, with light radiating from Him. I felt like I was surrounded by a love I'd never experienced before, as I gazed at Him, a love so beautiful, it was beyond description in our capability.

With Mary and Denise kneeling beside me, I was aware Mary had her head bowed. I could hear her crying and telling the Lord how hurt she felt about her husband leaving her. On the other side of me was my sister-in-law who had experienced such joy from being set free from her sins and heavy burdens. Her hands were raised up as she worshiped the Lord. Jesus was not looking at me but at Mary, and His expression changed to sorrow as He saw her crying out to Him. He didn't speak the way we speak to each other with our voice, but through my spirit, I heard Him say to her, "I know your pain of being rejected; I too have been rejected by those I love; I will be with you and comfort and bring you through this, and I will never leave you or abandon you."

Then He looked past me to Denise. As He watched her, His expression changed again; He began to rejoice with her. He didn't say anything to her: He was just enjoying the freedom she had to worship Him. He was not looking at me, but I believe He was saying, "This is not about you; it's about the message I'm giving you for My people. Go and tell people how much I love them. I took all the ugliness of their sins on my body for them. Not one thing that happens to them—no evil, no sin—was not on My body as I hung on the cross. Tell them I conquered death, hell, and the grave so they could have life everlasting with Me. Tell them I will never leave them." After that He just disappeared.

I knew Jesus was calling me to minister His love. Transfixed, I couldn't move or say anything for a long time, I was so full of God's love. Later while we were eating lunch, I told both girls what I had seen and heard. They were amazed and overjoyed that God had been there for them. It especially comforted Mary, because she was hurting so bad. They knew that I was telling them the truth. They trusted my love and fear of God.

CHAPTER **11**

My Husband's Transformation

I was walking on cloud nine for a week. My husband knew there was a dramatic change in me: he saw the joy and zest for life I had. There and then he decided that, whatever I had, that was what he needed. So at the end of the week he came to church with me and went forward to ask Jesus to be his Savior. Right away there was a change in him also. He loved to go to church, and some of the men his age began to mentor and bond with him.

Like me, my husband grew up without being taught about God. When he saw how the Holy Spirit moved in the service, he too believed that God was still doing supernatural signs and wonders on earth, and he wanted to be a part of it. Ted began to pray that Jesus would fill him with the Holy Spirit. He didn't receive the heavenly prayer language right away; instead he went on for weeks praying about it. That caused him to doubt and think God did not want to give it to him, or that something was wrong with him. But the Pastor and some of his new Christian friends kept encouraging him.

Then it all happened one Sunday when the message was, "Is there something in your life that is more important than God? If there is, this will keep you from receiving God's blessing because of the condemnation you feel about yourself." The Pastor went on to say, "Whatever you find comfort in other than God, give it up, give it to the Lord and He will set you free from it."

Holy Spirit Power

I was later to learn that because the Baptism of the Holy Spirit is a gift, people who feel condemned about something they are doing or have done in the past do not feel worthy to receive it from God. This is interesting because they know salvation is a free gift from God, and believe they are saved through Jesus' sacrifice for them. They know it was nothing they did to earn it. And yet they think the gift of being filled with the Holy Spirit is something they must strive for by trying to be being holy. The truth is no one has the ability to live a holy life, set apart for God, without giving the Holy Spirit full control.

Again, a lot of people are taught that they receive the infilling of the Holy Spirit the moment they accept Jesus as their Savior. That may happen with some people who know what the scripture says about being born again and filled with the Holy Spirit. It also may happen to a person who, at the time of their acceptance of Christ has asked the Lord to take total control of their life, and for God to use them. But, just as the original disciples of Jesus had to be instructed by Jesus on waiting to be empowered by the Holy Spirit before they preached the gospel, so must most of us know what God's word says, and in faith ask to be filled with God's Spirit. The people who have been taught that there is no interval between "being born again," and being filled with the Holy Spirit, usually do not expect a second experience of being empowered. Only the Spirit of God has the power to carry out His work through us to make Jesus not only our Savior, but also the Lord of our life.

It is hard to give complete control over to God, especially when we have not surrendered our tongue to Him. The Word of God tells us the tongue can release blessings or curses, and it exposes what is in our heart. In water baptism, the biblical way is to be completely submerged in water. It is the same with being filled with the Holy Spirit—we need to be filled to overflowing with His Spirit. We can't ask Jesus to fill us up partly and tell God He can't control our tongue; this shows we are not trusting in the Lord, or fully surrendered to Him.

God chose a sign He would give us to show that we are filled with His Spirit: a new language that we haven't been taught. We use that language, besides our natural language, to pray and worship Him. He chose that new language because it comes direct to us through the Spirit and bypasses our minds. That's the Spirit of God Himself speaking through us in the language of angels. This gift of tongues helps us to pray for a need we don't know how to pray for. So praying in the Spirit will help you when it's too hard to pray in your own understanding. Walking in God's Spirit will also help you conquer the demands of the flesh, and the temptations satan and his demons set up for you.

Now being filled with God's Spirit is not a one-time experience. You must stay filled if you're going to live by the Spirit and not by the lust of your flesh. You will then be able to do mighty works in the name of the Lord. But you have the choice of whether you want to stay filled and keep walking in the Holy Spirit or not. Just think about this: if you're drowning and someone throws you a lifeline, but you don't grab a firm hold of it, then of course you will drown. Jesus throwing you the lifeline of salvation has pulled your head above the water, and saved you from drowning. But you must hang on to the lifeline of being filled with God's Holy Spirit until you get to the shore. The Holy Spirit will protect you through the authority of Jesus Christ from the water (the world) filled with sin and sharks (satan, demons) that are swarming around you in the water waiting to devour you.

After the Pastor gave the message, quite a few people went up to the altar. Some took packs of cigarettes, and placed them there in surrender. My husband walked up and put his cigarettes on the altar. He even said to the Pastor, "I'm giving my addiction to God." Before he could even finish his sentence, the Pastor put his hand on my husband's shoulder and suddenly, my husband began to speak in another language. The congregation began to clap and rejoice with him. The Pastor hadn't mentioned in his sermon that smoking cigarettes was a sin, but because there was starting to be so much news about the harmful effects of cigarettes, that brought conviction to my husband. He loved smoking as much as I did. He knew that in his heart the reason he wasn't stopping when he felt convicted to do so, was because he didn't really want to give it up. But at this service he knew the Lord again was asking him to give up something he loved more than God. He finally decided he needed God more than the cigarettes, and trusted the Lord to take care of this addiction. And, of course, the Lord did. It didn't take him seven days like me. That day, he was to walk out of that church never to pick up a cigarette again.

The next week there were even bigger changes in him. He was so excited and wanted to attend church every day the doors were open. He got involved with the men's ministry at church, while I became one of the regular ministry workers at the coffee house.

CHAPTER 12

All My Children

I finally persuaded my foster daughter, Ann, to come to church with me on weekends and I would take all my children. The children enjoyed the Friday night ministry. They liked the music and especially liked that we would go out to eat afterwards. Although Ann went, she didn't make any move toward God. In the meantime, Social Services asked me if I would take in another teenager. It meant Ann would have to share her bedroom. Even though Social Services gave us money for room and board, it was very little as many times the girls came with just the clothes on their back. I always spent more money on the teens than Foster Services provided. I didn't want my foster daughters to go through more rejection than they already had being poorly dressed when starting a new school. And God supplied the extra I needed.

As usual, they didn't have a home to send this fifteen-year-old girl to. She would turn out to be the most abused child I would ever foster.

Judy had been in and out of the foster system since she was a small girl. Her home life was one no child should ever have. I won't go into detail, but by the time she was fifteen years old she had run away from home many times. She went through a cycle of not going to school, ending up in court, and being sent to another foster home. Her mother would blame Judy for all her problems and tell the court she couldn't handle her. Through the years I don't believe Judy told the court everything that was going on in her home, or they would never have sent her back.

Her mother and brothers were all she had and, no matter how she was treated by her mother, she always wanted to live at home. Like many kids from broken homes, she thought her mother didn't love her. For a long time, Judy tried to please her, but when it didn't work, she became angry and would argue with her mother. She still felt it was her fault that her mother didn't love her.

It was no wonder that by the time Judy came to live with me she had many emotional problems. At times she would revert to another personality if the emotional pain was too much. Judy also made up stories about her past, stories of another girl who had a wonderful life; at these times she seemed very happy. The court had required her to go for counseling, but it didn't seem to help. Counseling was ordered for most of my foster children, but I couldn't see any change in how they felt about themselves, nor did any solutions they gave help them. Their answer was medication.

It was a good thing my own children were so young because I spent a lot of time after they went to bed talking with the two girls. I treated the girls the same as if they were my own children and felt that way toward them too. I really believed God was expressing His love for them through me.

Judy's Escapade

My first foster daughter Ann never gave me any trouble. She was always respectful, even though I didn't think she liked going to church. My new foster daughter, however, even though she was always respectful to me and obeyed me to my face, would make plans to do something sneaky behind my back. She had been in trouble for running away with her boyfriend before she came to live with me, so the court said she should no longer have any contact with this boy. Yet, without telling me, she gave him our home phone number. He would call when she had told him the times I would be out of the house, or she would call him.

One night while we were all asleep, she got up, got dressed and took my car keys and, in the freezing snow, "borrowed my car," as she put it, to go to see her boyfriend. There, of course, was a big problem—and it wasn't just stealing a car—she didn't have a license and she didn't know how to drive.

For some reason I woke up, went to the kitchen, looked out the window, and noticed my car was gone along with Judy. I knew I had to call the police, or she could be killed or kill someone else. I also knew Social Services would take her from my home because that's what they did in foster care those days. Even if I wanted her to stay, the court won't allow it. But I had no choice but to call the police and the Social Services emergency line.

Thirty minutes later, they found the car and Judy in the ditch. She hadn't got very far. She was taken to the police station, and Social Services came to pick her up. She was to go to court in a couple days. Her social worker said, "There is no hope for her to go back as, once a foster child does something illegal while living in a foster home, the judge will automatically send her to a juvenile home.

Even though I understood why they had that rule, I was so upset, because I knew she didn't realize that her impulsive action would take her out of my home. Like any teenager, she thought she was in love, when she had never known what real love is. When I got to court, Judy told me how sorry she was that she took my car. We sat down on a bench outside the courtroom waiting for her time to go in. When Judy heard her social worker tell her she would be going to a juvenile home, she started to cry. "There is nothing we can do to change the judge's mind," the social worker said

I put my arm around Judy and said, "What do you want to do?"

"I want to go home with you," she said.

"Well, the only one who can change the judge's decision is God. Do you want to pray for that to happen?" I asked her.

"Yes," she said. We bowed our heads and asked God to move the judge's heart to allow her to come home with me. I knew if we asked in Jesus' name, the Father would grant us our request according to His will. Soon we were called in. The social worker said that I would not be allowed to speak. I thought that was odd. Shouldn't the foster parents be able to say how they feel about what happens to the foster child?

The judge seemed in a hurry as he had a lot of cases that day. After looking at Judy's case work folder, he asked Judy's social worker what had happened. She told him the whole story. He had Judy stand up in front of him. "Judy you can't seem to get along or follow rules in any foster home you have lived in. Stealing your foster parent's car, you could have killed someone or yourself. You need to be in a place where you must follow the rules, so I have no choice but to send you to a juvenile home."

"Oh, God, no!" I thought.

But just then he looked over at me, "Do you have anything to say about this?" I had prayed that the Holy Spirit would give me the right words to say if I was allowed to speak.

"Yes, your honor, I do. All her life Judy has known nothing but rejection and abuse. As you know she has been in and out of foster homes since she was a little girl. She has experienced such terrible things for a girl her age, it took years for her to learn to respond the way she does now. Healing for Judy will not happen overnight, but I would like to be a part of that healing."

The judge looked at me with a quizzical expression and said, "You know you're right. I'm going to give her one more chance to stay with your family." He looked over at Judy, "You'd better be thankful that your foster mother is willing to forgive you, but this is the last chance I will give you, I don't know why I'm doing this. You may go home with your foster mother."

Judy was relieved beyond words. She had already had a taste of detention and couldn't wait to get away from it. I asked her on the way home, "You know, God did this for you?"

"I know," she said.

The Lord showed His love and power to my first two foster daughters and to my children many times. Even though I took the girls to church and the coffee house, neither of my teen foster daughters surrendered their lives to Christ at that time. I prayed for them every day; even years later I continued to pray for all the children put into my life. I knew the Lord was the only one who could heal their hearts and, like I had told the judge through the Holy Spirit, it would not happen overnight.

Ann's Dark World

My first foster daughter, Ann, was deeply involved with dark spirits when she came to me, although she was unaware of what they were doing. I knew that, before she came to live with me, Ann had been very much involved in the drug culture of that time and listened to dark music that glorified the devil. This left her very open to demonic influence. These evil spirits would even use her to threaten me and try to convince me they were more powerful than God. One day as we were driving together down the road, I was sharing some things Jesus was doing in my life, and how Jesus had power over the devil. Suddenly out of the blue Ann said, "The devil just told me he can make your car go off the road." Before I could say anything, my car for no reason, started to swerve off the road. As I pulled back on the road visibly shaken, the Holy Spirit rose up in me, "Satan you're a liar from the pit of hell. You will leave this car, and you will not speak to Ann again, in the name of Jesus Christ."

Ann didn't say anything more as we drove on. We were both shocked at what just happened, and I tell you, I was just a young believer then and wasn't any great woman of faith. Satan had just spoken something to Ann, and she just repeated it, but the Holy Spirit spoke something to me as well, and I repeated it. Guess who is the stronger of the two? The devil never used her to threaten me again. Believe me, this was just a step to teach her who God is and the power of His name that can destroy evil spirits and the devil himself.

Jennifer's Narrow Escape

Another time, I had to go to a meeting, and Ann said she and Judy could mind my three-year-old daughter. They had both been with us for quite a while and had not gotten into trouble for a long time, plus both girls were doing well in school. It was now summer, so they were on vacation. I would be gone only a couple of hours; besides, my mother was home next door if they needed her. Ann especially was motherly with my three-year-old, and I wanted to show the girls I trusted them. So I said "Okay."

As soon as the meeting was over, I headed home. When I walked in the door Ann ran up to me with Jennifer in her arms, "She's not breathing," she said panic-stricken.

"What happened?" I asked as I took Jennifer from her arms.

Ann explained they gave her popcorn, and while she was running around, she began to choke. Ann tried to dislodge the popcorn, but when Jennifer stopped breathing, she tried CPR. I also tried to dislodge the popcorn, but it wasn't budging. I knew there wasn't time to call an ambulance as our town no longer had one, and the nearest hospital was thirty minutes away. So, I told the girls I was taking her to the hospital. They jumped in the car with me; Ann held Jennifer, trying to get her to breathe as I drove as fast as I could. Ann said, "I don't think she's going to make it; she's not breathing at all."

In panic I yelled out, "God, please heal my daughter." When nothing seemed to be changing in her, I began to pray in another language. I knew at that point the Holy Spirit was interceding for my daughter. He was calling out to satan to take his hands off Jennifer in Jesus' mighty name. As soon as the Holy Spirit was done praying through me, Jennifer broke out in a loud cry; up to then she hadn't made a sound.

"She's breathing," Ann said excitedly. We pulled into the emergency room parking lot and rushed in. The doctor examined her right away and said she was fine.

He said, "From what you described, the popcorn had lodged in her windpipe, but had somehow dislodged.

"We prayed," I said. I don't think the doctor believed she had not been breathing for so long. There was no permanent damage because God had healed her completely.

On the way home, I told the girls it wasn't their fault. They didn't know they weren't supposed to give popcorn to a three-year-old, let alone allow her to run around with it in her mouth. I also know they were curious about me praying in another language. I told them that the Holy Spirit was praying for Jennifer. I explained this was one of the gifts for when a child of God needs to pray for something and they don't know how to pray. I also told them that the Lord let me understand that what I was praying for in that different language was why Jennifer was alive and healed: it was the Holy Spirit that had intervened. I knew the Spirit of God was using these moments as God moments in Ann and Judy's life, just as those moments had happened in mine as a young girl.

This would not be the only time satan would try to destroy my youngest daughter; God had a mission calling for her and that made her a target. She was close to four years old, when she woke up in the morning and said to me, "I had a dream."

"Oh, what was it about?" I asked.

"Jesus was up in the sky, and you were with Him. I asked Jesus if I could come up with Him too, and He said, 'Come.'" I was amazed she was so clear about what she saw.

Not long after that, the older girls were all in school, I had to counsel a few women and asked my husband if he would mind Jennifer for me, as he was off from work that day.

"Sure," he said. I really didn't like to leave her with him, because he sometimes would fall asleep on the couch, and not pay attention to our toddler. But they had gone outside to the backyard, where he was cleaning up the yard and she was right beside him playing.

Just before I started to leave, I looked in the backyard through the kitchen window. Jennifer was on her little Wheelie, still right by her dad. A few minutes later I walked out to my car parked by the side of the house, towards the front with the backyard no longer in sight. I started the car up and at the sound of the motor starting, my husband looked around and realized Jennifer was no longer with him. In a panic he began to yell for her and ran around to the front of the house. I had just put my car in reverse and was about to push my foot down on the gas pedal.

I didn't hear him yelling but caught a glimpse of him running to the side of the house with his arms waving at me. Immediately, I shut the car off, knowing something was wrong. I jumped out of the car, just as my husband was heading to the back of my car. I was chilled to the bone at what I saw: my daughter on her small tricycle was right up against the back of my car. I would never have seen her, as she was so much lower than my back window. I didn't get over that for a long time.

The enemy of our soul was trying to kill two birds with one stone. He would try to get rid of Jennifer (who would later be called to Asia as a missionary), and thereby try to wreck my life and emotionally stop my ministry. He was constantly trying to put fear in me about my children, but I kept them in my prayers for the Lord's protection over them. He was showing me not to fear, for He had the children covered. After all, they were only loaned to me to raise, love, and know Him, but they belonged to Him. Satan couldn't have them, or destroy them, because by faith I had already given them back to God.

CHAPTER 13

Long Time Fears

In the process of my growth, God began to deal with some long time fears. As a young girl I had developed a fear of storms and a fear of flying. Even though God had already shown me how He was more powerful and bigger than me when I was a little girl, I was still afraid of storms. It especially didn't help when we had our first horrible tornado in our area that killed and injured many people. The news showed a body that had been flung up against an electrical post, which scared me very much.

Every time there was a bad storm, I would think there was going to be a tornado. Even if there was no watch or warning, I would take my children to our basement. It really upset me that I still had that fear after becoming a Christian. I felt I wasn't trusting in Jesus enough to protect me and my family. I kept praying about it, asking God why I had this fear.

One day while praying, a picture came to my mind, that of a little girl hiding under a table, when it was storming outside. The Holy Spirit spoke to me, "That girl is you, and because your parents did not know Me or have a relationship with Me, they could not comfort you with wisdom."

When He said that, I remembered how my parents made fun of my fear. All they would do was laugh and say, "There's nothing to be afraid of."

But the Lord said if they had known and trusted Him, then they would have told me at a young age not to be afraid because the Lord has control of the storms. All I had to do was ask Him to protect me. If my parents had trusted Him and felt He had that much power, it would have helped me get over my fear. It was wonderful for my Father in Heaven to explain it like that, but I still couldn't control my fear when a bad storm came.

That Sunday I went to church in turmoil about my unbelief and fear of storms. I did not want that fear to rule my life anymore and wanted the Lord to help me get rid of it. I had tried so hard to overcome it myself, but it wouldn't go away. The Assistant Pastor gave the sermon this Sunday and he was also used by the Holy Spirit to speak on the Gifts of the Spirit, especially the word of knowledge and healing. During the altar call the Pastor gave a "word of knowledge." The word of knowledge is a supernatural gift to a person to know something that would not be known to that person. Its purpose is to help someone.

So the Assistant Pastor called out, "Someone here has an uncontrollable fear, and God wants to deliver you today." There is no way this man could have known that about me, as I had not shared it with anyone at the church. I knew without a shadow of a doubt that was for me. I knew there was a demonic spirit tormenting my mind. It could not own my spirit that belonged to God, but it could invade my mind, since I had allowed it to dominate my thoughts. This demon was lying to me to make me doubt that God could help me with my fear, whereas the Lord wanted me to believe His word and not satan's lies.

I got out of my seat and walked up to the Pastor, "I'm the one you're speaking about, I need prayer."

He looked at me, put his hand on my shoulder and said, "You spirit of fear, you will not speak to her again, in the name of Jesus Christ!" As soon as he said that, I stepped back as if something pushed me; yet it was not the Pastor. I fell to my knees, knowing I would never have those tormenting thoughts of fear control me again. I worshiped and thanked the Lord. I'm not foolish: if there's a warning of a tornado coming my way, I will take precautions, and ask God to protect me, my family and the people in that area. I am not going to test the Lord foolishly. But I do not panic when a storm comes.

The Test

It's funny that, even though I no longer have an uncontrollable fear of storms, I still had to deal with the fear of heights and claustrophobia, that is, being enclosed in small spaces, like airplanes, and elevators. I think my biggest fear is not being in control in these situations. For so long I felt there was no one that loved me enough to protect me, so I had to control everything in case I got hurt. That morphed into many things I thought would harm me. Fear and faith cannot live in the same space. I felt that these fears stemmed from my own feelings of feeling unloved; this would be my "thorn in the flesh," a persistent issue that Paul too was irked by. But God was going to deal with these fears by showing me how much He loved me and would protect me if I trusted Him. In other words, I was going to walk in faith, believing in God's love and strength for me the rest of my life, especially in these areas where my emotions were tempted to fear.

So, what is the first thing the Lord asks me to do as a newborn baby in Christ? Get on an airplane, of course. Since my husband worked for the airlines, we could travel on standby anywhere in the world for free, but since we had been married, I had refused to fly. Now that I had given my heart and life to Jesus, my refusal would not be acceptable to God.

After my second foster daughter had come back to live with us since the car incident, things had settled down for a while. Now Social Services decided she needed a wake-up call because she had been in so many foster homes, and her mother wasn't ready for her to come back home. So they chose to send her to this new program which the American Government had coordinated with an organization in the United States that operated an orphanage in Haiti. Some teens that were not adapting well in foster homes were chosen to help in the orphanage.

Life was hard in Haiti. My foster daughter did not want to go, but Social Services wanted to try out this new program to better help these teens mature. I knew this would not help my foster daughter, as lack of material things wasn't her problem. Lack of unconditional love was.

Judy was distraught about going. I told her that once she was there and needed me to come, I would go visit her. To tell you the truth, I was trying to pacify her; I really thought she would never ask me to come there. Not two months later, I got a letter from her saying she was very depressed and would I please come and visit her? "Oh, no!" I thought. I wrote back to her that I would see if I could make arrangements. I knew that if I didn't go, she would think everything I told her about how God and how I cared for her were lies. Choosing to trust in the Lord over my fear, I prepared to leave.

We had been flying for a little while and I was having a nice conversation with the pilot's wife, seated in front of me. Suddenly, the plane began shake violently; it seemed like it was dropping. I was scared to death. "My first trip, my children and I are going to die," I thought. "God, what is going on?"

Just then, the pilot came on the intercom, "We've run into some pretty bad storms, folks. Make sure your seat belts are on; we should be through it shortly."

The pilot's wife said, "This area is known for bad storms, but I've flown a lot and never experienced turbulence this violent."

Of course that did not calm my fear. I just prayed, "God, please stop this dropping and shaking of this plane, in the name of Jesus Christ!" To my surprise it stopped immediately. I know it wasn't because of my great faith, but I was so scared and desperate, at that point I knew He was the only one who had the power to help us. There's something about being in a completely powerless situation that will make us cry out in desperation to the Lord. And God honored His name and answered me. I was so relieved when we landed at our first stop, Puerto Rico.

The kids and I enjoyed the ocean and the beautiful surroundings of the hotel. But I kept thinking about having to get back on that plane again, and how much I hated the thought of it. I really think God was showing me great mercy. I had been someone that walked with Him a long time, and He had answered all my prayers. Nevertheless, I still walked in unbelief when trouble came. I was no better than the Israelites, who after being set free from Egypt and seeing so many miracles on their behalf, still couldn't trust God. Later in my life, He would show me mercy again over my unbelief in certain times of testing. God was strengthening my resolve not to obey my fear, but to trust Him. The unbelief no longer controlled me when I chose to believe and obey God.

Two days later we were on the plane again headed for Haiti. It seemed everything was going smoothly, and we were not far from landing. As the plane was descending, I could hear the landing gear going down. As that was happening, from my window seat, I thought, "Wow, we were coming awfully close to a mountain." People were looking puzzled too. "What's going on now?" I thought. I could feel my body tightening up as I looked out the window. But suddenly, the plane started climbing again. We already had our seat belts on and the pilot made no announcement.

We were now moving up and away from the mountain, circling around, and then we began to descend again. I was meeting the head of the mission organization at the airport in Porte-au-Prince. She had been at the terminal watching the plane come in, and after we finally landed, she said to me, "I haven't seen any plane come that close to a mountain before!"

The stay in Haiti was an eye opener for me. There were shacks everywhere, and hundreds of children begging in the streets of Port-au-Prince. There are poor areas in the United States, but compared to Haiti, the poor in the United States would be considered middle-class. When the cruise ships pulled into the port with their tourists, the children would surround the people coming off the ships. I was told by some of the locals that the parents sent a lot of these children to beg, because it was the only means for them to feed their children. Others were street children that their parents had abandoned.

The Mission Administrator said we would have to take a cab up the mountain where the orphanage was. I don't know if you could call what we rode in a cab; it was a very old car that felt like it would fall apart any moment, and there was barely enough room for the four of us and the driver. We started up the mountain and right away I noticed the road seemed really narrow with not enough room for two cars on the curve.

I asked the Administrator, "What happens if there's a car coming from the other side? He's driving so fast!"

She spoke to the driver in his language, and turning around to me, said, "He said, 'One of us goes off the road and dies.'" The driver turned his head around to look at me and laugh.

Keep your eyes on the road; this isn't funny, I thought.

I was told the Haitian life expectancy at that time was only forty, so he may not have expected to live long anyway. As for me in my early thirties with two of my children with me, I was not ready to die. I must admit, my faith had dropped to a low point; between the battle of getting on the plane and now this. Battle fatigue was setting in.

We finally made it up the mountain without the car falling off the cliff, with the view of a beautiful retreat and orphanage ahead. My foster daughter was very excited to see us, and I had missed her. It's funny how especially my first two foster teens felt like my daughters that had been born to me. I know that was God's love He put in me for them.

The first thing Judy said to me was that she wanted to go home. I explained to her that I couldn't make that decision for her, since she was under the family services and court's jurisdiction. She would have to complete the program which had about four months to go.

Even though the ministry there was wonderful for what they did for the children who were orphaned, it was far different from her life in America. She had to be up very early to start the day, and help prepare food for the children. After that her workday would begin. The retreat had a large garden, where they produced food for the orphanage. Judy would have to work in the garden, and help clean and take care of the orphans. She had been used to a very undisciplined life, like many American teenagers partying with friends much of the time. Eventually they sent her back to the States early. Even though she was given plenty of free time after work, and the people in charge would plan many activities and trips for the teens from the States, this young lady just could not adjust.

As we toured Haiti, it seemed that poverty was reflected everywhere, except for the luxurious grounds of the Haiti President's mansion, walled on all sides. Haiti has a natural beauty about it, but it was all the shacks and dirt roads, animals running everywhere, unsanitary conditions, including the food, that obscured its charm.

I dreaded getting back on the plane again to the States. I was flying standby, so I couldn't schedule a flight to fly straight through, and we had to stop in Miami for a layover. The ride to Miami was up to now uneventful, so I had started to relax a little. But as we started to approach the airport in Miami, the pilot came on the intercom, "Sorry folks we're having a little trouble with the landing gear; it should be fixed shortly."

My body began to tense up at once, "God, you've got to be kidding!" I said out loud, and I didn't care who heard me. "Help us, Lord, please keep us safe, in Jesus' name!"

After a few minutes the landing gear went down, and we proceeded to land. When I stepped off the plane in Miami, I was shaking like a leaf. This was not helping me lose my fear of planes, but I thanked God for bringing us through it. I was beginning to think, maybe I was going to have to take the attitude of the three Hebrew boys who were put into the fire; maybe I would have to go through danger to see that Jesus is always the fourth man in the fire, and whether I live or die, He is with me.

The rest of the journey to Michigan was without incident, for which I was very thankful. In my mind, though, I didn't want to get on a plane ever again. I would have loved it if I had been delivered from my fear of flying, but satan wasn't going to let it go that easily. God had plans for me, plans that required that I be able to fly. These are times God expects us to be overcomers and walk in His strength. God would expect this of me in this area the rest of my life. So, the Lord allowed satan to try and stop me from going on these trips. God was very patient and merciful in putting up with my arguing or begging Him not to require what He was asking me to do.

I learned later that putting off what He wanted me to do could be a matter of life or death. It could mean a person dying before making their peace with God and being sure of their salvation. I learned this the hard way when I delayed going to share the gospel with someone God had directed me to. It was a neighbor and she died of a sudden heart attack that very day. While I was hesitant because of fear of rejection, God was to show me how important it was to obey when you feel the urgency to do what He asks of you. He forgave me but I cried over it for a week.

CHAPTER 14

Foster Teens Going Home

Eventually both girls would be sent back to their homes by Social Services. But they never really left me; they would always remain part of my life.

Judy's Experience

Judy's social worker called me one day and said, "Once Judy comes back from Haiti, I think she's ready to go home. She seemed to be doing well at your house; she has stayed out of trouble for a while." "Do you really think she should go home?"

"Her mother has expressed to me she doesn't want her to," I said.

"I know but she's doing so well, and our purpose is to reunite them with their families," she said.

"I understand that, and that's what I want also, but her mother has refused to go for counseling. She thinks everything that has happened to Judy is her fault." I argued.

"Well, I'm going to try it and see how it works out between the two," she replied.

She sent her home the following week. Judy was overjoyed, of course, still hopeful that her mother would love her because she was good. The problem was that her mother, who had been abused by her own family growing up, didn't know how to love herself or anyone else. I tried to keep in touch with Judy after she left. The last time I had spoken to her, I had to meet her a little way from her house. She said she was okay—but I didn't believe her. She looked like she wasn't getting any sleep. After that I didn't hear from her for a few weeks.

I called her mother, and she said she didn't know where she was. Another week went by, and I decided to call Children's Services. I was starting to worry, but the next day I got a call from the hospital asking if I was Judy's foster mother.

"I'm her former foster mother," I said.

"She's here in the hospital in a serious condition and she's asking for you," the doctor said. He wouldn't tell me anymore. I jumped in the car, driving a little too fast.

I couldn't even imagine what I was going to see. She was lying in her bed hooked up to every conceivable machine. She looked so gaunt and malnourished; I didn't realize what was under her covers that covered her stomach was the reason why.

"Judy, what happened?" She tried to talk to me, but they had given her pain medication, and I couldn't understand her.

The nurse came in, "The doctor would like to talk to you. "

"I'll be right back," I told Judy and followed the nurse out down the hallway into a small office.

The doctor got right to the point. "Judy was admitted here two weeks ago with a gunshot wound to her stomach. She was unconscious when she arrived here and had to go immediately into surgery. The first week we didn't know if she would live. When she became conscious, she was able to give us your number and wanted you to come to the hospital

"Is she going to be okay?" I asked.

"She may never walk again or be able to have children."

I continued to visit Judy at the hospital and pray with her. She told me what happened, "I was depressed and wanted to die. I got one of my brother's guns and shot myself through the stomach."

I asked God for a miracle for her, that the doctor's prognosis would not come true. He answered that prayer and the other prayers from the coffee house and church who were also praying. He answered big time. Not only can Judy could walk, though with a slight limp, she is also married with children.

Although God performed so many miracles to show Judy how much He loved her, she couldn't get over the anger and unforgiveness towards those who had hurt her. She still wanted love from people who, without God, weren't capable of giving it to her. She would have to face more misery and tragedy in her life before she would open her heart to God. I saw how she was taking the same path I had taken for some twenty years.

God would teach me through Judy to love unconditionally the way He does. Judy was the one person for whom God gave me such a love; nothing she did could shake that love for her. Of all the teens and children I have fostered, Judy had been through the most abuse, it was a miracle she survived. Even though I had trouble with her stealing my car, and not wanting to go to school, she would open up about her feelings of hurt and rejection. I felt that with God's help, even though it might take years, she could be healed by God's love.

It's so amazing to me that children who have been terribly abused physically or emotionally still want to go back to their abuser, especially when that abuser hasn't changed. I learned that these children have been raised from birth to accept such abuse as a kind of love. Since they haven't experienced real love, they are uncomfortable around someone who is expressing real love and caring for them. They don't believe it's real or that they deserve it.

So, they act out their bad behavior to try and get the foster parents to reject them, proving that they deserve it because they are unlovable. They are so used to rejection, that, when the opportunity to go home presents itself, they choose to go home, especially if they've been in foster care for a short time. The fact is some foster homes are not much different from their own homes. I have kept in contact with Judy on and off over the years, although we both moved away to different States. She is now married and has two children and grandchildren, whom I'm also grandmother to.

Ann's Deliverance

The opportunity came for Ann to go home as well. I felt she wasn't ready, but it had nothing to do with her parents, who I knew wanted her home. I felt she should stay with me till she finished school. She didn't need to be around her old friends who were still into the drug culture. Her parents hadn't changed either, so she would still be looking for validation from her friends and boyfriend. She would be turning eighteen the following year, and she would not be expected to sit under her parents' rules.

I kept in touch with her. Since she rejected God's love for her at this point, after she left for home, she began to get more and more entangled in the drug culture of her friends. It wasn't long before I lost touch with her. Her parents said she had run away, and they didn't know where she'd gone. I began a prayer vigil that lasted over a year, asking God to protect her and bring her to surrender to Him.

One day I received a phone call from her. "I'm back in town. Can I come over to see you?" she said sounding desperate.

"Of course," I said. It wasn't long before one of her friends dropped her off at my house. As we sat at my table, like we'd done many times in the past, she told a harrowing tale of what had taken place in the year she'd been gone. She had hitchhiked to Florida and got involved with a group of people involved with witchcraft. The things that began to happen scared her. She broke loose and hitchhiked back to Michigan. While she was talking, I was thinking, "Thank God, He had me pray for her every day!"

In Michigan she immediately got involved with the wrong people again. She was invited to a biker party by one of the men she met. At the party they were drinking, and playing loud rock and roll music. Her friend was saying something to her, but she couldn't hear him. Suddenly, a man across the room shouted at the man she was with, "Bastard I'm going to kill you!" as he pulled a small gun from his pocket.

Everyone shouted, "Get down!" while the man she was with shoved her down, just as the bullet whizzed past the two of them.

All Ann said she could remember was thinking "I have to get out of here!" She got up and ran out the door. She didn't know what happened at the party, but she kept running along the dark country road until she came to a well-traveled road, and hitchhiked home. The next day she called me. Sitting at the table she told me, "Dolores, I'm scared. My life is a mess; I really need help."

"Ann, you've chosen to go your own way. I can't help you—but Jesus can," I said.

There just so happened to be regular meetings on Friday night at a ministry for young people our church had started. It was in a barn called The Jesus Barn. Each week there was a different speaker. This Friday as the speaker was a young man who had been in prison. He was out in a friend's car, waiting for him to come back from robbing a convenience store of money and alcohol. His friend ended up shooting and killing the store worker and both men were arrested. This young man was around eighteen at the time, and sentenced to jail as an accessory to murder.

In prison, he gave his heart to God and began to minister to the inmates. He had asked God to set him free, and if He did, he would continue to be a prison minister if the Lord wanted him to. So, the Lord showed him favor and had him released early. He kept his promise to God—not only did he minister in prisons, but he traveled all over the United States speaking to young people.

"Ann, would you like to go tonight and hear his story?"
I asked.

"Yes," she said. I kept her at my house the rest of the day.

When we arrived, the barn was already full of young people and we had to sit way in the back. There were no chairs, and everyone was sitting on the floor. The music and worship started. The young people were very exuberant in their worship, jumping up and down, dancing, and clapping to the music. The music and words by the young group were saying, "How powerful and good God is, even to deliver those that are broken hearted, and bound by satan!"

I thought, "Wow, God! How appropriate for Ann to hear this!" That was nothing compared to the real story she was about to hear. She would hear a story about a young man who was bound in his own prison before he ended up in a physical one. Satan had long tried to destroy this man's life before he became an accessory to murder. He told them that in prison he was so remorseful for the man who had died. "I never went to that store with the intention of killing anyone, but I had made a choice to go with my friend that night, knowing what we were going to do was wrong." He couldn't have felt more guilty for what he had done; but it was too late. He couldn't take it back. He was miserable and wanted to die but was scared to die. What was beyond the grave? "What if something worse is waiting for me?" he thought.

Satan began to torment him saying, "You need to kill yourself. You are worthless. Even your family doesn't love you or come to visit you. You are a disgrace to everyone." It's a typical ploy of satan to set in for the kill when someone is emotionally crushed.

I listened to him tell his story, thinking, "Ann, God is here to meet you tonight!"

The young man went on speaking about how one of the inmates asked him to go to chapel with him. At first, he didn't want to go. Then he thought, "What do I have to lose anyway? I've already lost everything. I don't care what the other inmates think of me, I'm going."

He told the audience, "The music calmed me. I hadn't felt such peace for a long time. The Prison Chaplain stood up and began to talk about how God had sent His Son to give us new life and how He went through rejection and torture to pay for our sins. In that way our debt to the Father would be paid, even though He had never sinned." While the chaplain was speaking, the young man thought, "Why would He give His life for my sins? I've done nothing to deserve it?"

Just as that thought crossed his mind, the Chaplain said, "And we've done nothing to deserve this payment for our sins, nor is there ever anything we can do to deserve it." He thought, "You mean this is free, and all my guilt will be wiped away if I accept Jesus' payment for me? I didn't even wait for the chaplain to stop speaking. I ran up to him, with the room full of inmates, and cried out, 'I need Jesus!' I dropped to the floor. I could hear many inmates praying for me; it was like I was in a dream. At the same time, I felt something leaving me, as if releasing me."

He continued, "At the same time, the chaplain bent down to me and asked if I wanted to ask Jesus to take over my life. I said, yes, and I began to ask Jesus to forgive me, and to come into my life. 'I want to serve You the rest of my life.' Then something so deep and so hard to find words for happened. I felt so clean, like a newborn baby. I have never felt loved, but now the kind of love I felt was in me and all around me. I looked at the inmates who had been praying for me with a love that I knew didn't come from me, but God was filling me with love for them. They were all rejoicing for me.

"I would spend a few more years in prison learning the word of God, learning how to forgive people who had hurt me, and ministering to other inmates. And God graciously answered my prayers about leaving prison before my time was up. So here I am, doing what I promised Him I would do. I know there are some young people here, bound in sin just as I was. How do I know that? Because God wouldn't send me anywhere, unless there was someone here that needed Him and was seeking Him."

After the speaker said this, he invited those that wanted to surrender their lives to Jesus to come up to the makeshift altar in front. There were quite a few young people who walked up there. But Ann wasn't moving. I asked her if she would like to go up front to receive Jesus.

"No, I don't want to go up there," she said, shaking her head.

"Don't you want to receive Jesus?" I asked.

She bowed her head and very quietly; I could barely hear her "Yes."

"Ann all you have to do is ask Jesus to come into your heart and forgive your sins, just like the speaker did. Just say the words ..."

She started to say, "Jesus come ..." then she stopped and looked at me in despair. "I can't."

"Why can't you?" I said. "You said you wanted to accept Him."

"I don't know, I just can't say the words."

So, I opened my Bible to Romans 10:9 and asked her to read the scripture.

"That if you confess with your mouth..." That's as far as she got. "I can't read it," she said. The rest of the scripture read: "... the Lord Jesus and believe in your heart that God has raised Him from the dead, you will be saved."

"Why can't you read the rest?" I asked.

"I don't know," she said, shaking her head and looking as frustrated as I was.

As I was talking with her, I was unaware that the speaker had been walking up to us. When I looked up, he was standing right beside us and asked, "What's wrong?"

"How does he know there's a problem if he was so far away from us? He can't possibly know," I thought. "And there were people at the altar—what made him leave them?"

I turned to him, "I really don't know," and that was the truth. I was a young believer myself and had never seen anything like this before. I continued as I looked at Ann, "She wants to accept Jesus, but said she can't say the words."

He was standing beside Ann as she sat on the floor. He reached over and rested his hand on her shoulder. "Don't be afraid, I've seen plenty of this in prison. I'm going to pray for you. Is that okay?"

She nodded her head. I expected him to start praying as we bowed our heads, but instead he just stood there with his eyes closed—which seemed like eternity. Finally, I looked up at him, and he looked at me. "I'm waiting on the Holy Spirit," he said.

"Wow," I thought, "this is new!"

Right after saying that, he startled me as he began to address the devil and his demons saying in a loud voice, "Satan, you have no authority here! You lying spirit from hell, leave this girl now, in the name of Jesus!"

Suddenly Ann stood up and said, "I love Jesus," with both arms raised in the air. As she said it, I saw something leave—either by my spiritual or natural eyes—I really don't know. When she stood up and was about to speak, I saw this vapor leave her mouth. Again, I thought, "I have never seen anything like this before."

Ann was overjoyed and couldn't stop smiling. Ever since she had come to live with me, she had this sad look. On the way home as we talked, I could see this look of peace and amazement on her face. The smile couldn't seem to leave. I asked her why she couldn't pray the prayer of salvation before.

"Thoughts kept coming to my mind about how stupid this was, and that it's not true that anyone can change their life. The thought also came that these kids were fools. It wouldn't stop and I couldn't concentrate on praying."

I told her that it was the lying spirit that the man of God prayed to leave her, in the name of Jesus Christ. He prayed in Jesus' name, and the devil knew he had lost his power to have this lying spirit stay. Afterwards, Ann would eventually go home and rekindle a relationship with her parents. Ann would eventually marry the young man she had always been in love with. They both left their drug lifestyle behind them and went on to be wonderful parents of beautiful children.

My foster children taught me a lot about hurting people. Neither of them believed I loved or cared about them just because I said so. Each child was an individual with different hurts and anger. I had to treat them like they belonged to me, just like my own children. I had to be always fair, and not show favoritism. I spent time with each one and developed a relationship with them. I had to show my love by disciplining them when they were doing something that would hurt them.

Above all, I had to value them more than anything else in my life—just like the rest of my family. Then, just maybe, they would see God's unconditional love and the love of the Holy Spirit expressed in my life. And, just maybe, they would see they could be forgiven, loved, and given a new heart too. I learned from my experience with these two teens that it was the answer not only for me, but also for all people who have been crushed in spirit by sin.

CHAPTER 15

Our Coffee House Ministry

I had been working in the city coffee house for quite a while now and my first foster teens had returned to their homes. I kept feeling like God wanted me to start a coffee house ministry in our small town. I knew there was a drug problem with the young people, and even though the public school was trying to address it, they were not successful. I knew that Jesus was the answer, but I didn't know how to start a coffee house ministry or any kind of ministry outside of foster care. Yet it would not leave my mind. Every time I prayed, it would pop in my mind, and was sometimes there even when I wasn't praying about it. Then something else began to happen.

New Coffee House

Every time I would drive through our small downtown café, I was drawn to this small vacant building in the heart of town. The Spirit of God would say to me, "That's the one for My coffee house."

"But I don't have any money to rent a building," I thought. My husband made good money, but we were still paying for our home, two cars, plus all the expenses a family with children had. "This can't be you, Lord," I would say. But He wouldn't let up. Thank God I was reading scriptures every day and getting great teaching from the church about how God provides for us when we trust Him with our tithes and offerings. I learned right in the beginning that the first fruits of our income belong to God and, even though my husband and I agreed on tithing, I still didn't move on the leading of the Spirit of God about the building. I was too afraid to step out in faith. Thank God He knew I was still a baby in spiritual things.

One day an old school friend of mine called me. I was surprised because I had heard she had married and moved to California. "Hi Dolores, long time no see!" She went ahead to tell me she now had two children and that they had moved back because she was divorcing her husband. I told her, "I'm sorry to hear that. I'm a Christian now. I have given my life to God."

"I have also become a Christian," she said. "Even though I got a divorce I didn't want one."

"Her husband must have done something really bad to her," I thought. I knew God hates divorce and didn't allow it except for adultery. She asked me if I would like to meet for lunch because there was something she wanted to talk to me about. "I would love to meet you for lunch! I'm excited about learning how you became a Christian!" I told her.

We met a couple of days later. She hadn't changed much – she was a nice-looking woman and had a sweet personality.

She told me she had felt so empty and disillusioned with life, like my own reasons for turning to Christ. But then she said her husband did not turn to Christ. He didn't want any part of Christianity, nor would he attend a church with her and the kids. She said she was sick of his attitude and didn't like the influence he had on their children about church. "Has he said that he wants to leave you?" I asked.

"No, he thinks everything is fine. He doesn't mind me going to church and doesn't see a problem with him staying home."

Immediately, I knew she didn't understand God's word. But when I wanted to say something to her, the Holy Spirit stopped me and said, "I will take care of this. She is still a baby, just like you." So, I said nothing about her marriage.

Her next statement floored me. "The real reason I came back home was because God has asked me to start a ministry for young people in our town and He has already shown me the building He wants me to start it in."

The Holy Spirit quickened my spirit and I thought, "Uh oh. God got tired of waiting for me and got someone else to do His work." I didn't tell her anything about God telling me to start a ministry, but I did tell her how the coffee house ministry I had been saved in would be a great ministry for youth in our town. I also told her I would be glad to help her. She got so excited and asked me if I would want to ride by the building.

"Sure."

I already knew what building it would be without her telling me anything. I didn't ask her any questions about it. As we drove downtown, she pointed out the same building the Spirit of the Lord had shown me. I wasn't going to tell her about what God had shown me about the building until later. I felt I had disappointed God, and I didn't want to take away any excitement from my friend's obedience. She would be the one to start this ministry and I would help. The only problem was she didn't have any extra money for rent either. This time though, I knew it was God who was speaking to me about this ministry. I told my friend I would look into the building the next day and see what they wanted for deposit and rent. I also told her God would provide for it since it was His ministry.

The next day I called the owner of the building and we met there. When he told me the deposit and rent per month, I knew it was too high. I told him what I wanted it for and that we couldn't pay that much, as we'd have to depend on donations. He said he would get back to me. I thought he wouldn't call back. I called Kate, my friend from California, and asked her to continue praying.

"It doesn't look good, but if God wants that building, He will work on that man's heart tonight." I had a sleepless night because I was excited about the potential of what God wanted to do in our small community, but I was still a little apprehensive about the building. The Lord had to remind me that He had shown the same building to my friend as He had me.

"Stop doubting," He said in my spirit.

I waited all day for the owner of the building to call. Just about when I was ready to give up hope, the phone rang. I learned to call this "faith testing;" it was God's way of teaching that patience and expectation produce faith.

The owner said that because we wanted to open it for young people, he would cut the price in half. I knew this was God. I knew the rent was much higher in that downtown strip. To put the frosting on the cake, he also said he would not need a deposit. "Lord, you're amazing!" I thought.

Emboldened by His actions already, I stepped out in faith and said I would bring him a check the next day. I called my friend, who was so excited to hear this, but I still didn't have any extra money. This may be hard to believe—even then it was hard to believe—but on the way home I picked up my mail at the post office. In the mail was a letter addressed to me with no return address. I opened it and saw the rent money with a note saying, "I was praying, and God told me you needed this." The letter was not signed, but it was stamped from a town I didn't know anyone from. Only Kate and I knew about the rent money we needed. I asked Kate later if she had told anyone, but she hadn't because she wanted to wait and see if we had it or not.

I didn't know anyone in my town who played Christian music, so I asked some friends at the coffee house ministry in the city if they would come out on Saturday night and minister in song and the word. They were excited about the opportunity. Kate and I went about getting donations of tables and chairs. Some of the guys from the city came and built a small stage for us.

Ministry Beginnings

Soon after the coffee house was opened, another old friend from school came by. She lived out of state and was home to see her mother who had been sent home from the hospital to die. This mother and daughter had a strained relationship for years. The mother had been very abusive to the daughter as she grew up. As soon as she graduated from high school the daughter left town and had not seen or talked to her mother in years. The daughter had recently become a Christian and had come to visit her mother on her deathbed to tell her she loved her and had forgiven her, and that Jesus loved her. She asked me if I would go along with her.

As we entered her bedroom, I remember the room being dark with the drapes closed shutting out the daylight. Her mother was lying in her bed with her eyes closed. "Mom," the daughter called out, and her mother opened her eyes, "It's me, Pat. How are you feeling Mom," Pat asked? Her mother was silent, I had the feeling this daughter was still very fearful of her mother. She went on to say, "Mom, I'm so sorry you're sick. I love you, Mom. Jesus loves you too and can heal you."

Her mother turned her head and looked at her with nothing but pure hatred in her eyes and said, "Why the hell are you here?" Then out of her mother's mouth came the vilest ugly words toward her daughter. I was shocked and we were both speechless.

Pat ran out of the room weeping. I stood there for a second thinking how weird that I had prayed for this visit with her mother. It never came to my spirit to pray for her now, as if what was set was set. Pat and I walked outside. I prayed with her, and told her to let me know if I could help in any way. A couple of weeks later Pat stopped by the coffee house and not only shared with me her mother had died, but how she died. She said she and some of her extended family stood by her mother's bed. Her mother, who hadn't spoken for days, had been staring at the ceiling, and suddenly turned her gaze to a corner of the room. With a look of sheer terror she began shouting at the corner, though no one was there, "Get out of here, you can't have me, I won't go!" She closed her eyes, and began saying in a trembling voice, "My feet are burning." She kept repeating it until she took her last breath.

Her daughter again told her mom, "I love you." Pat told me all the time she stayed with her mom, until her death, her mother never spoke to her.

Even though I was young in the Lord, I knew from reading God's word that the mother who was dying was entering hell. But the Savior had sent her daughter to give her one last chance to be saved from the hell. Now she was choosing to enter hell and had rejected His mercy. The daughter left town grieving for what could have been. But at the same time, she had peace, because she had forgiven her mother, and felt Jesus' love for her. All the years she had hated her mother had left her and been replaced by God's love. She had wept for her mother as she also knew Jesus was weeping for her. Because she knew she had forgiven her, she was free in her own heart of the hatred and bitterness she had lived with for so long.

When I walked out of that home that day, and after Pat told me how her mother died, I knew this short time we spend on earth is no game. Everything the Spirit of God had spoken to the prophets through the ages about Himself, about us, and the purpose for our life here and eternity is true. It has, and it will come to pass. The Holy Spirit allowed me to witness this incident to share how serious the decisions we make are, and how merciful God is. Even up to the last moment of life on earth, He is ready to forgive us. It reminded me of the sinners crucified beside Jesus. One accepted His mercy, the other did not. My prayers for my family and friends became much more urgent, especially for my own parents.

One afternoon a young man walked into the coffee house. I recognized him as the younger brother of the bully who had knocked me off my bike when I was younger on my way to my grandmother's. Both brothers were still troublemakers in town so, at first, I thought he had come in to make trouble. I hoped he hadn't been drinking because he could become really mean then. I was glad my husband had come in after he got off work. This young man didn't come in to start trouble, though, and in fact he was in a battle for his life. One part of him wanted to know about Christ but the other part of him was controlled by a demon. I asked him to come and sit down so that we could talk. He sat down beside me, and my husband stood over to the side of us.

I could tell this young man hadn't been drinking. "Would you like a cup of coffee?" I asked.

"No, I want to know if God is real," he said. I knew then he was searching for God and that the Holy Spirit had led him into the coffee house. I began to explain the gospel to him. He was very receptive at first. I shared some of the miracles I and others had experienced, but when I started to share how he could pray and ask Christ to be his Savior, he became agitated, and his voice changed.

He was looking at my legs and said, "You have a snake crawling on your leg." I was taken by surprise and looked at my husband. My husband hesitated for a moment and then said, "Satan, in the name of Jesus, be quiet." Immediately, this man's expression and voice went back to normal. My husband and I had seen many people delivered from demons, drugs, alcohol, and religious spirits through the coffee house and church ministries we attended.

I again started to talk to him about accepting Christ. He at once turned and looked at me with the evilest of expressions. He took a knife out of his pocket that happened to be a switchblade. As he put it up to my neck, he said in the most unearthly voice, "I will kill you." I didn't have any time to think or be afraid. I was immobilized and in shock.

Suddenly my husband yelled, "In the name of Jesus Christ, you demon of hell, go back from where you came!"

The man got up, pushed his chair back, and ran out. To say we were both shaken was an understatement. We didn't call the police but instead prayed that he would get deliverance. I didn't see or hear about him until years later when we heard that his older brother had cancer and was dying. Both brothers had given their lives to Christ.

The coffee house was open all week except Sunday. We offered free coffee and pastries, a library of Christian books, Christian counseling, and bible study twice a week—one at lunch, one at night. Saturday night was our big night of ministry with praise and worship, testimonies, prayer, and joyful fellowship.

The odd thing was that, even though we thought that the coffee house would be a ministry to young people, the people who were stopping in during the week and on Saturdays were people in their twenties and forties. Some who came on Saturdays loved it so much that they became regulars. People that came were either those who didn't attend church and were searching to know God or others who attended different churches and had questions about our beliefs. Some who had been studying Scripture on their own came to believe in being filled with the Holy Spirit and speaking in God inspired languages was of God, and wanted to understand it more.

Quite a few people coming through our doors were searching to know the truth. Some who already had church homes and had received the baptism of the Holy Spirit tried to tell their pastors about it but were told not to talk about it to anyone in their congregation. And some were told by their Pastor they should leave their church. Of course, these pastors believed what their denominations taught without a personal study of the word of God or asking the Holy Spirit to reveal truth as they studied.

As the ministry at the coffee house was growing, I became more and more concerned about my brother. He seemed to be falling deeper and deeper into darkness. My sister, sister-in-law and I were praying for him; then God called my sister-in-law and me to fast for him. One night, as I was alone in my room kneeling and praying for my brother, I remembered a dream that God had given me as a child of my brother, David, in a deep pit filled with snakes. I didn't understand until I had given my heart to Jesus that those snakes were demons trying to destroy my brother.

As I was kneeling and praying, I began to feel a presence come into my room. I started to shiver. It became like a cold, damp, musty, smell—almost like an old house that had been unoccupied for years. Fear started to grip me. On the wall, across from my bed, appeared a vision of the earth, and I was looking at it as if I were in a spaceship. Across the earth appeared Chinese characters. Instantly, I knew they stood for the number 666. Then in the vision, I saw my brother bowing down to the number 666. Then a demonic spirit said to me, "Your brother is mine and will worship me."

For some reason, I couldn't say anything except, "Jesus! Jesus! Jesus!" At that point, the demonic spirit, the vision on the wall, the smell, and the cold left. I cried out to the Lord for my brother and the Spirit of God gave me a special measure of faith. He said, "Your brother will believe in Me and be saved." Even though it looked like he would never come to believe over the years, I could never doubt what God had told me.

Things began to change rapidly with the coffee house. Kate and I both took turns in the early part of the ministry working there during week days. We both had children, and I also had a husband and new foster teens to take care of. Since I had other teens come into my home after the first two, I tried to be home when school let out, so I could start dinner.

I kept asking Kate about her husband. She said he was calling her and asking her to come back. She said she wasn't going back. It was hard not to say anything concerning scripture, so I just said, "Oh."

Time went by. One day Kate surprised me. She had talked to her husband the night before and he told her that he'd been asking God why she had left. He had started reading the Bible and saw where it says, "When men and women marry, they become one flesh. And divorce is only for unfaithfulness."

Kate said they had a long talk, and she began to see how wrong she was. She told him that she would come back to

California, but he said he would fly out and drive her and the children back. She also said that she felt God was ending her time with the coffee house ministry, and that her ministry was now to her husband and children. "I also believe God wants you to continue the ministry," she said. I let her know how grateful I was for her obedience to come to Michigan, and for God to use her to give me a second chance at a ministry that would be a part of my life for many years.

I also was grateful to the Lord for trusting me again after I had failed him. Kate's husband, true to his word, not only flew to Michigan to get her, but he gave his heart to the Lord at a small church in our town. They went back to California. It did leave me with a problem, though. I still needed to take care of my family and I would not be able to fill in for Kate at the coffee house. But God was way ahead of me because He had already made plans for that. My husband, who in the beginning didn't want anything to do with the ministry, began to want to spend more time there, which was a great help to me.

We were getting more and more people coming, and quite a few men were really on fire for God. My husband began to form a relationship with these men, and it helped him to stay focused on Jesus and the exciting things the Holy Spirit was doing in our small group's lives. After a while, the men began to talk about the fact that there was no church in our town that believed the full gospel, especially the work of the Holy Spirit. The closest one was thirty miles away, which was the Assembly of God that we attended. They asked what my husband and I thought about starting a church in our small town. At the time, there were only about three churches in town. My husband thought it was a good idea. I knew we weren't called to pastor at that time, and I loved my church in the city.

We decided to take the question to Pastor Snook. My husband called him, and they set up an appointment for the people from our coffee house, the Senior Pastor, and Assistant Pastor to meet. We let the people who had been attending our coffee house share their desire for a full gospel church in our town. Pastor Snook listened and then said that he thought it would be a good idea since there were so many small towns around us that had no full gospel church. He said he and Pastor Lobbs would go back and pray about it. And if God gave the green light, then they could initiate the process.

I had no idea about the process of planting a mission church through a denomination; I left all that all to the men and the pastors. I was sad that my family and I might have to leave the church and people we loved in the city. It didn't take them a long time to decide. Pastor Snook called my husband and told him they not only had decided to go ahead with it, but they would send Pastor Lobbs to pastor our new church.

Pastor Lobbs met with the people who wanted to be the first members and formed a board with them, and they decided to rent a larger building as the coffee house building was small. My husband was one of the board members. I became a teacher to teenagers. One of the guys, Gordy Aikin, from another community about fifteen minutes from us, had been a part of our coffee house ministry. He'd been in a rock n' roll band before turning his life over to God. He began to minister in our church and years later would become the Pastor of our church.

One of the people who had come to our coffee house to ask about the ministry of the Holy Spirit, Cliff Thurlow, was a music leader at his church. He now felt God was asking him to come to be a music leader at our church. So, he and his family moved to our church, and he was our music minister for several years. The church grew quickly under the Holy Spirit ministering through Pastor Lobbs. There were many signs and miracles. People were having dreams, visions, being saved and healed, and having financial miracles. It was an exciting time. The people were so dedicated to being used by the Holy Spirit in leading others to Christ that we grew rapidly and soon needed a larger building.

The men decided to construct a new building. When they found the land they wanted to build on, the price was too high, and the landowner did not want to come down. So, one Sunday, Pastor Lobbs took the church over to the land and we marched around and prayed that God would give us favor with the owner to come down to what we had offered, which was a reasonable price. A few weeks later the owner agreed to sell us the land at our offer price. He said he changed his mind because his parents were Christians and when they had left him the land, they said they wanted the land to be used for the Glory of God. Every night and weekends, the men would come to the site and work. Of course, satan tried to stop the work. The church was almost built, but one day, we had a terrible storm and the roof was blown away.

But the men went right back to work. Nothing was going to stop them from building this church because they knew God was in it. Once the church was built, the people loved going to church so much, that one day in spite of a bad snowstorm on Sunday morning when all the roads were shut down, a few of the men who had snowmobiles went around picking up people who wanted to go to church.

Pastor Lobbs and his wife, Lois, taught us the meat of the word of God. He was such a man of God and teacher that many of us grew to be strong Christians. Many went into ministry. Our children grew and matured in the Lord. Many were saved and filled with the Holy Spirit at a young age. My four-year-old daughter had a dream where she saw and talked to Jesus. Our middle daughter was about nine years old when she went to a retreat for young girls. She had given her life to Christ earlier and now received the Holy Spirit and spoke in a new language as the Spirit gave utterance. She came home so in love with Jesus and so excited. Many of the children gave their hearts to Christ and received the Spirit through this wonderful children's ministry taught by Gordy Akin's wife, Cookie.

One day my oldest daughter, my husband and I were driving home from a Sunday night church service. My daughter was sitting in the back seat, leaning up against the back of my seat talking with me. I noticed how big and bright the full moon was that night and said," Wow! Look how big the moon is!" Suddenly before she could answer me, my daughter and I saw the moon burst into flames. I looked at my husband, "Did you see that?"

"See what," he asked.

"The moon just burst into flames."

He was driving with a full view of the moon from his front window, yet had not seen anything. I knew God had shown my daughter and me a vision, but it really scared my daughter. In my spirit God told me to read her Matthew 24. I had my bible with me, and did not remember what was in Matthew 24, so as I opened it up to the scripture, I soon realized it was one of the signs Jesus spoke about concerning the end times and His second coming. This scripture mentioned there would be signs in the sun, moon, and stars.

The Spirit of God had spoken to me at different times about the last days and His second coming—to expect it to be soon. Now He was now speaking to my oldest daughter about it. There were so many supernatural visions and dreams that young people experienced in those days of the early coffee house ministry and church planting, which would be too long to relate.

As for me, I loved teaching teens; they were so eager to learn. I taught from my own study of the word of God and my own experience, letting the Holy Spirit lead me in what He wanted taught, not some pre-prepared teaching material. I know that denominations do this to help teachers who do not feel confident, to make sure the teaching is the right fit for different age groups, and that there is no error. It's just that I wanted to get the text for the day right from the Bible and the Holy Spirit. The Holy Spirit is the one who calls people to ministry whether they are teachers, prophets, apostles, evangelists or pastors. He is the one who both equips them, and gives them the messages to teach.

All the same not everything was wonderful and peaceful. I soon learned after our new church started that God was going to teach me something about humility. At one Sunday school class, a couple of the girls asked me about speaking to their father since their mother had refused to let them see him. They said their father was an alcoholic but had been sober for a while. I asked them if their mother and father were divorced. They said they had been for a long time. They expressed their desire to visit with their father a little each week. Although the court had agreed, their mother refused and would get angry at them for asking. The girls said they had been praying to God about it.

I felt I could only tell them what the Bible said so this is what I said, "You must honor your parents. But it does make it difficult since both parents disagree. You should continue to pray and let God move in this situation and not get angry at your mom. Also, the Bible says that if you can't forgive your brother, you can't be forgiven. Pray that your mother can forgive your dad."

Well, the girls didn't do what I said about leaving it up to God. They went to their mother and told her she needed to forgive their father because that's what I had told them. The next service the girls sat in the adult service with their mother. The mother glared at me during the regular service. Afterwards, one of the girls caught me in the hallway and told me that her mother was mad at me, and that they were never to go to my class or speak to me again. I was devastated. I went home, cried, and asked God why? I didn't get an answer.

That Wednesday night at worship, this woman kept glancing my way with a disgusted look. I tried to close my eyes and concentrate on worship; usually after a few minutes of sacrificial worship, I could enter His presence and the world around me would disappear. But this time, I couldn't ignore the fiery darts coming my way. Again, I went home, got on my knees, and cried out to the Lord, "Lord, I can't even concentrate and worship You. How can she sit there during worship with such hate in her heart?" No answer from God.

This went on to the next Sunday and I'd had enough. When I went home, I felt I didn't want to go to church anymore if a Christian was allowed to act like that in church, but I didn't realize I was blaming God. I got on my knees, crying, praying, and telling God I didn't want to go to church anymore. This time, He answered me, but it wasn't the answer I wanted to hear. He said, "Go to her and tell her you're sorry if you offended her."

"But Lord, she's at fault here. I meant no harm. I only wanted to bring love and peace between the parents," I protested. He still said the same thing. So, I told the Lord that I would.

The next time at church, I went up to her before the service began, and said, "I just wanted to say how sorry I am if I offended you." She looked at me with pure evil in her eyes and said, "Well, it's about time. You need to mind your own business." Her girls were standing with her and looked away embarrassed. I stood there in shock not knowing what to say. She walked away from me. I could hardly get through the service that day and couldn't wait to leave. Again, I went home and cried.

I asked God how she could do that after I had apologized. He said, "I didn't ask you to tell her you were sorry because she would accept it. The reason you should do it is to give her a chance to accept it and for you to be set free from her condemnation. Now the guilt for her unforgiveness is completely on her." Then I felt the burden lift off me and the next Sunday I worshiped joyfully, conscious of no one but Jesus and my love for Him.

That day I learned a very valuable lesson. Even if someone intentionally hurts us, we are to forgive them, whether they accept our forgiveness or not. The scripture "forgiving a brother" doesn't hinge on their acceptance or not before God. It just hinges on our obedience to our Father and forgiving them, even if they are the ones that were wrong. There is real freedom in that. We are a forgiven people—even though we rejected Him. We are free to love and forgive because we have been forgiven. It wasn't soon after that incident that the mother took her daughters and left the church. I continued to pray for them but never saw them again.

As the church continued to grow, Pastor Lobbs felt God was calling him somewhere else for ministry. We were sent several candidates for the position of pastor, but none seemed to fit. The board had to vote on the pastor, and they couldn't seem to agree. In the meantime, people wanted a pastor and were getting impatient. Finally, a Pastor from out of state came just to fill in until we got a permanent Pastor, but the people misunderstood and thought he was eyeing the pastoral position. Even though this Pastor only wanted to fill in and liked where his family lived, God had other plans for him and our church.

After Pastor Hillsman gave his first message at our church, the people were in love with him and told the board members he was the man that they wanted, and that God had sent him. Of course, this was all news to Pastor Hillsman. The board asked him if he would be willing to take the position. He said he hadn't thought about moving his family from the state he lived in, but he was always open to God's direction and would pray about it. In the meantime, the board felt they needed to vote among themselves since they hadn't voted on him yet.

There were some who thought they should wait and interview more candidates, but my husband said, "We need to go home and pray and come back and pray again." When they met again and prayed, the vote was unanimous for Pastor Hillsman. They called the Pastor who had already left for his home and told him about the vote. Pastor Hillsman also had been praying and said he felt God was directing him to pastor our church. This was going to be quite a difficult move for his family. He had a wife and two teenage daughters. It was going to be a long trip from a warm state to a state with long stormy winters.

That transition was not only going to be hard, satan also wanted to stop him and his family moving. As they were preparing to move, his wife had a major attack of asthma and was taken to hospital. She couldn't breathe and the doctors felt she wasn't going to make it. Pastor Hillsman contacted our church and asked us to pray. We at once began a prayer vigil for her at church. Two days later she was sent home with no trouble breathing or any further asthma attacks.

We rejoiced and knew that God was sending this man to us, and nothing was going to stop him and his family from coming. Even though we were excited about the new Pastor, we were sad about Pastor Lobbs leaving. Pastor Lobbs knew and studied the Bible every day of his life. In all my years of serving the Lord, I have never met a pastor that knew the Bible like he did. His ministry calling was that of shepherd and teacher. A lot of us were very young in the Lord and even mature Christians had sat under leadership that didn't study or know the scriptures like this man did.

We were truly blessed to be taught by this anointed man and his family. For someone like me, who knew hardly anything about the Bible, the church, the Christian life, and the Lord I would be serving, we learned from him not only the basics, but also the deep things of God. This is the kind of teaching that makes you grow and become strong in your commitment to God. It's the kind that shows you the miraculous wisdom of God for His plan for creation and the wonderful plan He sets in motion for our salvation. This was something I would not hear in the many years to come of attending pastoral teaching from different churches, denominations, and conferences.

CHAPTER **16**

New Ministry

My husband and I had wanted to move to warmer climes for quite some time. I especially hated the winters in Michigan. For a long time I was content with the ministry and family of God that we were surrounded with. I dearly loved my church family as much as my own family, but we both were becoming restless, and after Pastor Hillsman was called to the ministry of another church, we felt God was calling us out too. I especially began to feel our work was over with this church.

We still had no idea where the Lord was calling us, but the airline that my husband was working for was moving into other states and smaller airports. Quite a few of the states were in warmer regions, even though it was a long shot to be sent to one of these states. A lot of the men with more seniority than my husband wanted to be transferred to warmer states; but we put in an application anyway. We were expecting something to happen as we knew we were called to home missions, which meant, after a church began to grow, God would move us to help or start a new ministry. But it happened so quickly it took me by surprise.

I was down in our basement sorting some clothes, when I heard very clearly the Holy Spirit say, "Get your house in order—you are about to move." Two weeks later my husband got a notice we were to be transferred to Valdosta, Georgia.

Valdosta, My Home

South Georgia was vastly different from the north in terms of culture, and also the weather. We flew down to visit Valdosta and my first impression was of the intense heat. It was like opening your oven door as the heat blew in your face. "Boy, it's hot here!" my husband exclaimed.

But I loved it. We were about to continue on the road of joy and God's favor. All I'd ever wanted to do growing up under cold winters and sometimes cold summers was to move. My body soaked in the heat, which could get to a hundred degrees in the summer. I knew it stayed warm pretty much most of the year, except for a couple of months in the winter, which, compared to Michigan, was like being in a tropical paradise. We rented a car and began to do some sightseeing.

I wasn't disappointed in what the Lord had whispered into my spirit. "You will like Valdosta—it's beautiful." After he said that, I looked up Valdosta in a set of encyclopedias we had. It said it was named by an Italian man who had named it after the area in Italy he came from called "Valle d'Aosta." It was graceful and lush with oak and maple trees, but it was the tall, pine trees that kept the area green all year. There were beautiful homes that were all landscaped with flowers I had never seen before. Later in the spring, the hot pink and white azaleas would spring up everywhere with purple flowers that looked like grape vines clambering up the trunks of the pines.

At the time, Valdosta College was a state teacher's college before becoming a state university. The beauty of this place was breathtaking with its tan stucco building and the roof tiles of red clay. "What a delight for these students!" I thought, taking in all the color of the azaleas bushes in their glorious array of color, crepe myrtle trees filled with pink, purple, and white flowers, white flowered magnolia trees and the pretty, white and pink flower dogwood trees, and of course the tall pines and palm trees surrounding the campus.

Except for a few short sojourns in Chicago, California, Florida, and North and South Carolina, I would call Valdosta my home for 42 years. No matter where I lived in my life, I considered Valdosta my home. We toured the large stately homes in the historic district, admiring the homes and city buildings that dated to the days of the prosperous old south and their cotton plantations.

The homes were so spacious in relation to the small families that lived in them. One of my daughter's friends had asked her to stay overnight. Compared to the average, three-bedroom one bath home we lived in, this was a mansion. It was so large that when my daughter left the bedroom to go to the bathroom, even though there were three bathrooms, she got lost in the house.

There seemed to be churches everywhere you turned. We found out we could buy or rent a house twice as large as the one we had in Michigan for half the price. The food was also so much cheaper than in Michigan. So were the taxes and the car insurance—your money went a long way in Valdosta.

Another thing we noticed were that strangers said hello to you as they passed you on the street and actually smiled at you. They waved at you as they passed your car. "Wow, what a friendly town!" I thought. It was something I wasn't used to in Michigan; there people looked away from you if they passed you, unless they knew you.

Stifling the Move of the Spirit?

We looked around for the first Assembly of God church to attend, as we were not sure in what direction the Holy Spirit would lead us in ministry. Just before we left Michigan, I attended a meeting where a missionary was speaking. After the meeting, as she was praying for people, she walked over to a table we were sitting at and started to pray over me. She gave me a word from God. "God is about to send you into dry land spiritually." That was interesting because I hadn't told her I was being sent anywhere. I didn't quite understand what this word meant, because we were about to move to the Bible belt! It didn't take me long to find out after attending the Assembly of God there a few times. It was a large church with friendly people and exciting worship, but so different from the Assembly in Michigan. The preaching was basic baby food, not the meat of the word. Even though they taught what the Bible said about being filled with the Holy Spirit and the gifts that flow, neither the leadership, nor the congregation allowed God to speak through them the way He wanted to.

Once a man in the congregation spoke out a word from God and the Pastor almost apologized for him. I knew then why people didn't let God use them. For the first few services,

I didn't have the Holy Spirit give me a message or a word of knowledge or wisdom for the congregation. I was used to God using me many times in speaking and in the prophetic gifts. I must admit I was a little fearful of being used in the church where the Pastor wanted so much control and not the Holy Spirit.

But it happened one Sunday morning, where the worship was so wonderful, and I was lost in the love for the Lord. Suddenly, I felt the Holy Spirit wanting to say something. I began to ask God to give it to someone else, but of course the Lord reminded me that I was putting my fear of man before my obedience to Him. On top of that, only one word came to my mind. I was going to have to step out in faith and speak that one word knowing that the Spirit would give me the rest as I began to speak. If I had not experienced this many times before and knew God would be faithful, I would have been petrified. So, I waited until the worship had quieted down so people would hear and it wouldn't cause confusion.

I had no idea what message the Pastor would deliver, but the Holy Spirit knew. And I was given a word for the congregation that would complement and bear witness to the Pastor's message the Holy Spirit had given him. Even though the Pastor allowed me to be used, he did not encourage the congregation to start letting the Holy Spirit use them. Again, I think it was that fear of losing control, or that things would get out of hand. It is so hard for man to trust God and so tempting to be a man pleaser (so that everyone will like them instead of God).

Through the years I've met many pastors who knew what the word said about using the body of Christ but were afraid they would lose some of their congregation if they allowed it. But that's the trouble—it's not their congregation, but the Lord's. It doesn't matter to God how big your congregation is. It matters if they have a heart of love for Him and want to obey Him. So many times, the church is run like a secular business, whose success depends on how many customers it has. But God's church is built brick by brick on the solid foundation of Christ the rock. If it is built on any other foundation such as numbers, it will eventually crumble.

And eventually that's what happened to this large church. At one service, the Pastor came out with the statement that he had built the church and wasn't leaving it. I don't know what was going on in that church, but I felt uneasy when he said it. What I had experienced with the Assembly of God in Michigan was that they moved their pastors around to different churches and the pastors themselves were often prompted to leave their church to minister in another, whether they had started the church or not. This was to guard against people following the Pastor and not Christ.

In due course, the Assembly began to dwindle. I won't get into all the conflict between the Pastor and his board, but he and his family left the church that he said he would never leave and got involved in another denomination. In the meantime, the position of Pastor had opened in a nearby town. Before the Pastor left this denomination, he asked my husband and me if we would be interested in taking that position. We said we would pray about it. We knew in our heart that God had sent us to Georgia to help with new works and not be a part of a large congregation. As we were praying about it, the Pastor's mother came up to me at one of the services. She was a very devout woman of God and would sometimes minister to people by the Holy Spirit. So, I asked her to pray about us taking the position in this town.

A Mission Church to Pastor

She didn't pray for me there and then. Instead she said, "Who knows but that you have come to this position for such a time as this?" I knew she was quoting what Mordecai in the Bible was saying to his cousin, Esther, when they faced a critical situation. I also knew in my spirit that was God's answer. So, the new journey had begun for our family to pastor a mission church. We were sent to a small town just fifteen minutes' drive from Valdosta to Quitman.

Quitman was what people in the south called "country," but I would call it one of the poorest towns in Georgia. We met with a man that the Pastor in Valdosta had told us about. His name was Alf Messer; he was the one who oversaw the church and, to my understanding, had started it, but had not taken on the pastoral position. I didn't know it then, but he would be one of the godliest men we would meet in our time in Georgia. We followed him a little outside of town to the church we were to pastor. We pulled up to a double wide mobile home sitting on a small grassy area.

This was the first time we'd seen a church started in a mobile home. There weren't too many mobile homes in the Michigan area where we used to live and certainly none we knew being used for a church. But the people we would pastor, as we would learn, came from an agricultural background like my father's and grandfather's and were very humble. The first service consisted of fourteen people, including our family of five. We became close to the whole family, as they were true Christians really dedicated to the Lord. The other family consisted of a mother and two children. Her husband didn't attend church.

That was the total size of our church, much smaller than the coffee house and church we had helped start in our town. But we didn't care about numbers. We were just so excited to have our first pastoral position. And so this small town some fifteen miles outside of Valdosta would become the town and the people we would fall in love with. Since I had grown up in a small town with a father who loved farming, I felt more comfortable with the people in this town rather than city folk.

I think at first the few people we had in church must have thought, "Why has God sent us these northerners to minister to us?" But it didn't take long for all of us to realize the wisdom of God because not only were my husband and I called to home missions (which meant we would be sent to start small works or encourage small works for the Lord) but these people were so much like us. I could see they were not interested in accumulating material goods or being successful in the eyes of the world, or about how large the church would become. We had come with a burning desire in our heart to teach Christ as the Head of the Church, and this small group had the same fire.

It's funny, even back then how the larger churches and organizations and some small churches forgot what God sent them to do on earth. It no longer was the Holy Spirit sending people out into the highways and byways, but it was church programs, skits, music, and dynamic teaching that they would try and use to draw people to church and Christ. People were constantly invited from the pulpit to ask people to attend this or that program, this music concert, or hear this message to get people saved. People forgot it was a one-on-one relationship of them loving the unbeliever and their families at their jobs and at school that would draw people to Christ and the church. It was the power of love. Sometimes that love and forgiveness would require great sacrifice on the believer's part. But people began to fall into the enemy's plan to get them to work from the flesh rather than from Holy Spirit power.

We had added only a few people when my husband felt we should move into a larger building in the downtown district, as we were a little outside of town.

We all prayed about it and agreed that greater visibility would help the people know the First Assembly of God church had come to town. A large restaurant had closed in town, and we felt this was where God was leading us. Since we didn't have many people and because we were a home mission church, my husband received only a small salary, which helped with gas, and the upkeep of our car. In other words, with so few people, we did not have much money, so God would have to give us favor with the owners of the building if we were to move. And the Lord did show us favor. The owner was willing to rent the space at a very affordable price and to hold off charging rent until we had finished all the renovations for a church.

The men quickly set to work painting, building a stage, and finding seats for the congregation. It was amazing how quickly it all came together. The people donated money and materials. After the new carpet was laid, we had a beautiful sanctuary and a church in a strip mall within reach of the busy highways.

And to top it off, we had a large parking area out front. The sign was put up on the building that welcomed people to our first church service. What a joyous occasion that was! We had many new people show up who were curious about the new church. We began to teach people what God said about everyone having a gift to share in the services. We taught how God sent the Holy Spirit to the believers to do the works of God and that He, the Holy Spirit, would prepare them for ministry to edify the body of Christ and bring lost souls to Jesus. They would very soon learn, especially as young believers, that they could do nothing without the power of the Spirit working in and through them. So many denominations taught that since Jesus had come, there was no need for prophets or apostles, and only accepted the ministry of the teacher, the evangelist, and elders/pastors. I sometimes wonder if this didn't fit into the idea that man could minister without the work of the Holy Spirit through the supernatural. My thinking about that was that man could speak words, but he couldn't produce the signs that Jesus had, which were supernatural.

I began to realize that although there were churches in the area that preached the full gospel, very few followed what Paul wrote in the 12th and 14th chapters of 1 Corinthians. These are about the nine gifts of the Holy Spirit to edify and encourage the people. In chapter 14:6, he asks, "What then shall we say brothers? When you come together, everyone has a hymn, or a word of instruction, a revelation, a tongue, or interpretation. All these must be done for the strengthening of the church."

Then, as you read the chapter further, you find Paul is not telling us these gifts and ministries were done away with after Jesus left the earth. In fact, Jesus had told His disciples to wait for the promise of the Holy Spirit "not many days hence." Now when the Holy Spirit came on the day of Pentecost, it filled them with a new language and supernatural gifts to reach out to people with the gospel with healings and miracles following.

But Paul was not only telling these new believers to let the Holy Spirit use them in the gifts, he was also instructing on the proper use of these gifts. Paul said through the Holy Spirit that everyone—the key word is "everyone"—when they come together, must do so for the strengthening of the church. The Holy Spirit working through the believer through gifts and ministry would be needed by the church until Christ returns, because the church would need building up. What could be the reason for church leadership presenting themselves as believing in every word of the Bible—and therefore calling themselves full gospel—yet denying the Holy Spirit freedom to move through the congregation as the Word of God said? I began to really ask God why.

In some of these churches you had to walk up front and there would be deacons standing there during worship. If you had a message, you had to tell them what it was before you were given permission to speak. But many times, if God gave someone a prophecy or word of knowledge or of wisdom, He did not give the full prophecy all at once; instead a word or prompt would come to your mind. But you had to step out in faith and, when you did, the whole message would come. In other words, it was coming from the mind of God, and not your mind. It was up to the people of God to judge the message, not one person, unless the message was given by God was just for that person's benefit. Just as we are to go home and study the scriptures to judge whether what the pastor, teachers and other ministers are speaking and teaching is the truth, against God's written word.

CHAPTER 17

More Upheavals

During the time our new church was growing, I was tested again with my old fears. My dad had called and told me one of my favorite aunts was in the hospital dying of cancer. I wasn't sure she knew the Lord and I knew she didn't attend church. As I was praying, the Lord said, "I want you to go to Michigan and pray with her."

Fear of Flying

"Oh no, not again!" I thought. I knew I didn't have much time to decide. I also knew it would not do me any good to tell the Lord "No," or hope that He would change His mind. So I prepared to go right away. This time I asked my husband to come with me, and I was taking my girls, as we would be seeing my extended family. I went through the same soulish battle with fear as before, but I knew there were no other options. I simply had to trust and obey the God I loved and who loved me.

The trip was smooth all the way up there. I went right to the hospital to see her with my father. She had lost a lot of weight, yet she still was a very beautiful woman. I greeted her and talked with her about the Lord. She said, "I have made my peace with God."

"The Lord can heal you," I said. He is still healing people just as He did when He walked the earth as a man."

"I just want to go home," she said. The doctors had told her she would not be leaving the hospital, because she was in such a bad condition. The cancer was throughout her body. She also said she wanted the pain to stop. What she was saying was she could believe God could stop the pain and get her back home, but she didn't believe He could heal the cancer. This was such a contradiction. But if we haven't walked with God and studied His word or seen or asked for miracles before in our own life, it's hard to get past what doctors tell you, or what your body is telling you. But the Father is merciful and will give us what we believe when we pray in His will and in the authority of His Son's name. So I prayed with her that God would take the pain from her body and allow her to go home.

On our way back to Georgia, we were to change planes in Atlanta to get to Valdosta. We had already boarded the second plane and it was fully loaded, when the pilot announced that it would be a little while to take off; they had a small mechanical problem and were working on it.

Immediately fear came over me. I wanted to tell my husband we needed to get off and take the children off the plane. But I knew he would think I was being foolish and letting my imagination run away with me. Since he had not been on the trip to Haiti with me, he hadn't experienced what I had. So, I sat on that plane till takeoff knowing something was going to happen to the plane, All I could do was trust God, even if we died on this plane. Shortly after takeoff, suddenly there was a big loud boom. I looked at my husband and he looked scared and so did everyone else on the plane, including my children. I told them, "Don't be afraid," and the weird thing was I was completely calm. Then a vision appeared to me.

Jesus was under our plane holding it in His hands. Then He spoke into my spirit, "This will be the smoothest landing you've ever had." I was so amazed and thankful. In the meantime, the pilot said we had engine failure, and would have to stay in the air to get the fuel off the plane before we could land back at Atlanta. My husband was worried about the other engine failing because of the strain on it, but I knew what God had promised, so I stayed calm. They were clearing the runway for us, and we were finally able to land. It turned out just as the Lord said, like landing on a cloud. When we disembarked my calm left me, and I began to shake.

We decided to rent a car to Valdosta, and one of the passengers decided to ride with us. He didn't want to get back on a plane either. As we were driving back, he told us he was sitting near the window where he could see the engine on fire. The thought came to him, "I'm never going to get home to my wife and newborn baby."

After I arrived home, I got a call from my dad. "The hospital had allowed my aunt to go home."My dad went every day to help her husband take care of his sister. He also said, "She is bedridden, but not in pain." I was so grateful to the

Lord for answering our prayers. She died a while later, the way she wanted to die in her own home, her own bed, with her family by her side.

As the church grew, we became a close-knit group, just like the church in Michigan. Our services were exciting with worship, healings, gifts of the Holy Spirit, and speaking and teaching that edified the body of Christ.

Whenever a ministry is effective in winning and strengthening people in Christ, the devil goes after it hard to stop it. That's exactly what happened in our growing church. My husband still worked for the airlines because we were called by God as home missionaries. We knew eventually God would send another Pastor to this assembly and we would be sent somewhere else. Satan wanted to destroy not only this growing church, but he also our family. There were quite a few things that were bothering me in my spirit about my husband. I knew from the time he was saved, he had trouble with walking in the Spirit and would give in to the demands of his flesh.

My Troubled Marriage

When we moved to Georgia and began to pastor, at first, he began to walk very closely with the Lord. I felt that he felt a deep responsibility towards the people he was pastoring. He seemed to have a genuine love for them and they for him. But as time went by, he became jealous of people speaking about how much they enjoyed a message that was given to me, as I sometimes would preach at a night service. I noticed he was not spending time studying the word or in prayer and was watching things on TV that were not proper for a Christian, just as he had done when he was first saved.

He became secretive and was always leering at pretty girls, just as he had done before he was saved. I noticed it even in church meetings, as we had a lot of young pretty ladies coming to our church. His sermons were beginning to sound empty because he wouldn't spend time with the Lord. He even asked me if I would write sermons for him. The final straw came when I walked into his airport office without him expecting me. He was with one of the girls that worked there with his arms around her. When they both saw me, they jumped away from each other with guilty looks on their faces.

He tried to make excuses but we both knew what he was doing. Our marriage and ministry went downhill from there. My husband did not want to admit he had a problem. He acted as if nothing had changed; he continued to pastor, but because there was no real repentance on his part, I was worried not only about our marriage, but about our church and how it would hurt the people who trusted and loved us. I was concerned about our testimony and what it would look like to struggling Christians in our church thinking that following Jesus doesn't make a difference in your life.

I wept and prayed many days over this. I didn't talk to anyone but Jesus about it. One day, God just took it out of my hands. My husband was notified by the airlines that they were moving us out of Valdosta and all employees of the airlines would be moved. That was a real shock, but I felt relieved. I thought, "Now the church can get a new Pastor that is not struggling with sin."

It wasn't long that my husband was moved to Hattiesburg, Mississippi. He said he would go there by himself and move us to Tallahassee, Florida and try to find work at the airport there. In the meantime, he would keep his airline job in Hattiesburg. For some reason, I felt we were not to move to Hattiesburg either, so we rented a house in Tallahassee. By that time, my oldest girl was married and finishing her education at UCLA. My middle girl was in college in Valdosta and my youngest was still in high school. Since my youngest was going to have to make the biggest change in her life, the Lord gave me the idea to start a sorority like one they had at Valdosta High School.

This would not be a closed sorority; it would be open to any girl that wanted to join, which was the reason the schools allowed me to start it. It was easy to start the sorority because the girls my daughter cheered with liked the idea and wanted to join. That was how God opened the door and made an easier transition for her to meet new friends. We gave parties with games and dancing and did projects to help the community. I know my daughter appreciated God's help.

During this time, my husband would fly home on his days off and put in his application to the Tallahassee airport and various airlines. We had been in Tallahassee less than 6 months when my husband lost his job with the airlines he had been with for years. He said they accused him of taking home the safety deposit box containing the money for tickets.

"I just brought it home for safe keeping," he said —but he knew the rules. That box was not to be moved out of the airport office. But he had lied to me so much; I didn't really believe him. Besides, the airline he was with had a union, and they would really fight for your job. So, I felt there was more to it than that.

Even though I didn't know it, I was about to go through a very difficult time again, a real time of testing. A journey on the road of sorrows again, but God's spirit would be with me all the way. Here we were in Tallahassee, with a year's lease on this house, and my husband jobless. I had been in ministry all these years, so I didn't have a paying job at the time. Our bills were beginning to pile up. My daughter had gone through all this transition and now this.

I cried out, "Why are we going through this, God?" and He answered me through His Word. One day I was studying and opened to Joshua chapter 7 which talked about a man sinning against God and he and his whole family were stoned to death for his sin. "What are you trying to tell me, Lord? My daughters and I are going to die for my husband's sin?"

He said, "No, but because your husband is the head and the priest in your home, you are suffering some of the effects of his sin. But just trust me—I will bring you through this in victory. Just continue to pray for your husband."

So that is what I did. It wasn't long before we were unable to pay our rent. I was looking for work, but nothing was opening. Shortly after that a couple from the church in Tallahassee offered to let us stay with them until we could find jobs, as my husband was still trying to get a job with a start-up airline out of Tallahassee. I knew all this was happening because my husband wasn't repenting. He even interviewed for a position of Pastor for another church but didn't get it. It wasn't long before I met a nice couple who said they would be interested in opening a gift shop about thirty minutes away from Tallahassee but didn't want to run it and just wanted to invest in it.

It seemed at the time to be the only thing that was opening, so I agreed to go into partnership with them. They would provide a loan with interest, and I would own it. They didn't know about any of my husband's problems but told me they would want me to run it and not my husband. The man had been in his own business before and now was a CEO of a large company. The sad thing was that, even though the gift shop was successful in the community right away and was making a profit, living off your profit for the first 3 years of your business is difficult.

You really need to be able to reinvest the money into the business. I was the only one working, so my hours were long and hard, but we still couldn't afford a place to live. It was hard on my youngest daughter since the people we were living with really didn't have enough room for us. I spent long nights crying and praying.

My oldest daughter and her husband that lived in California knew my situation. They offered to have my youngest daughter come and live with them and finish her senior year there. I thought it was a good idea, and her dad agreed. Shortly after that, my husband was hired for the small new commuter airline that had started up at the airport. That lasted only nine months. He was fired for sexually harassing a stewardess that worked for that airline.

Of course, he told me that she had lied about him. She was just mad because he had corrected her on how she handled people. I wanted to believe him because I desperately wanted to save my marriage. I didn't realize I hadn't left my heart open from God for any other choice. I made the mistake so many women make. It's really fear of failure— being afraid for the future for your family, and dependence on a man instead of God. The truth was I had become an enabler for my husband's sins and hadn't learned my lesson yet.

We ended up living in the back room of my gift shop with my youngest daughter having to start a new school in California. I knew she was in good hands with my eldest daughter and my son-in-law, but I felt so bad that she had to go through all these transitions all because of her parents, just like a lot of the foster teens that lived in my home.

I could not sustain the gift shop, so I talked to the man who had invested the money, and told him what was happening. I had already paid back a lot of what I owed him. He said that I didn't have to pay the rest back. He made so much money, he would take it as a loss, which would help him with taxes. I knew this was God's mercy. At the same time, my husband got another short-term job with the Tallahassee government. My daughter in California said we should move out to California and look for a job there. My husband suggested that I move out there first and as soon as his short-term position was done, he would move there also. I agreed. We were still staying in the gift shop and I missed my children.

We put all the merchandise in storage with our furniture. I thought that eventually I would want to come back to Valdosta. For some reason, it felt like that was where we belonged. I also thought if I kept the merchandise from the gift shop, I could restart the business. I was totally bound by the natural, making my own plans, forgetting God had called me to full time ministry, not trusting God or asking Him what He wanted me to do.

Because of all the trouble in my life, I became fearful. I felt things were getting out of control and I needed to take control so that my girls wouldn't continue to get hurt. I was blinded by all these feelings and apprehensions. I thought I was following God's will and was just a victim of other people's sins. Not only was I trying to take control, but I was leaving God out of my future. The Lord wasn't going to allow that. I moved to California and got a job in retail.

My husband's job was about to end but he kept making excuses about moving out to California. I had joined a church and became friends with the young Pastor there. I didn't tell him about my husband's trouble, only that we had pastored a church and he worked for the airline. My Pastor knew I was waiting for him to move to California. He also knew about my husband's job ending. I didn't know why but every time I went to church, he would ask if my husband had moved out here yet and I told him about all the excuses my husband was making.

One day he said, "Dolores, I don't want you to get upset but I think your husband is having an affair. This happened with my sister and her husband." When he said this, a light bulb went off in my mind and I knew what he was saying was exactly what my husband was doing. That night I called my husband and asked him if he was having an affair. For once he was truthful with me and admitted it. He said he had met her at his temporary job. All I said was, "I'm coming home!"

"No, I'm not ready yet," he said.

"What do you mean you're not ready?" Anger was building in me, the anger that was rooted in me as a girl. I thought, "How can you say that? It's not enough you've destroyed our family and your ministry. Now you want to destroy any hope of God saving our marriage?" I thought about my kids, especially my youngest daughter, who had already been through so much with her parents. "I'm coming home," I said and hung up.

I told my oldest daughter what was happening and said that I was going to go back, not to Tallahassee, but to Valdosta, where I had friends and relatives. I asked my oldest daughter not to tell my youngest daughter what her father was doing. I didn't want her to be in the middle of what was happening to her parents. I had kept a lot of things about her father from her through the years, knowing that in too many troubled marriages, parents use their kids against each other.

The biggest mistake a person can make in a relationship is to allow a person to abuse them physically or through unfaithfulness. Not only is it hurting you, and the children, if you have them, but you're also hurting the abuser by allowing them to treat you in a sinful manner. The Lord has a solution in His word on what to do. We are allowed to separate, but not divorce. The purpose of separation in this context is reconciliation and restoration. It is a time to be alone with the Lord, seeking His face and guidance. The separation is not freedom to seek comfort from another person of the opposite sex. I kept hoping my husband would change without giving him an ultimatum and that God would reach him. But I waited too long.

Looking back, I was more worried about what people would think. I did not save my marriage by allowing him to treat me that way—no one could save their marriage that way. He eventually left me to have affairs with multiple women, yet wanting me to continue staying married to him in case he decided to come back to me someday. He even came to the point of such deception that he could say, "Well, God allowed men to have more than one wife at the same time." Here was an example of a man who had been born again, filled with the Spirit, knew God's word, prayed with others to receive Christ, but had entered the dark place of the deceived soul. This was largely due to giving in to temptation and rejecting the Holy Spirit's conviction.

I moved back to Valdosta where I would have the support of my Christian family and friends. As it turns out God knew I would need their support. Moving back, living in a small apartment without my husband and children I had a lot of alone time, too much time to think. My anger turned into deep depression; old feelings of self worth came back, until I wanted to die.

But Thank God for my family and friends, He used to bring me back to the truth and reality, that God loved me and would get me through this crisis. God led me to apply for a job with troubled boys.

I prayed about what to do about my marriage as my husband was living with a woman in Florida. After I got back, I realized my husband had sold all our furniture, and gift shop merchandise and supplies to finance his dating as he wasn't making enough money to wine and dine her. It meant I had to start all over again. But again, God supplied all I needed.

I really felt no love for him as a woman to a man. Somehow, all the trouble and affairs had caused that kind of love to leave me, but I still wanted him to return to the Lord and I didn't want him to go to hell. But when I asked God about it, He said, "Dolores, I don't want you to divorce him. Even though you have every right to, I want you to give him time so I can work on his heart to return to Me."

"But Lord, I don't want to be married to him. I don't love him anymore," I said

"If I bring him back to you, he will be a changed man. I will not allow you to be treated like this again. And I will give you love for him," the Lord said. I knew that the Lord was able to do that, so I agreed. The only thing He didn't tell me was how long I would have to wait.

In my new job as a counselor, I really enjoyed working with the boys. Some were emotionally hurt; one had even killed his father to stop his horrible abuse of him. Since this was a Christian organization that the government worked with, I was allowed to share God's love and forgiveness with them. I sometimes spent hours comforting and praying with them. They were starved for love and God was the only one who could meet that need.

My husband during this time continued to have affairs and didn't seem to want to change anything. After two years went by, I began to question God about staying married to him again. The Lord answered me one day by asking me to call my husband and tell him I would be coming to Tallahassee to live with him. But he would have to promise me he would never cheat on me again. This was interesting because when the Lord had instructed me to move back to Valdosta after my stay in California, I was not to go to Tallahassee. My husband would have to move back to Valdosta in obedience with what

God was telling him. My husband wanted me to move to Tallahassee, but only to live separately, while he would be able to date me and others. So, I knew when the Lord had me talk to him about moving to Tallahassee to live with him that He was going to give my husband an alternative, in allowing me to go there. The day I called him, our daughter was visiting him. I said to him exactly what the Lord had told me to say.

This is the reply I got: "I would like to have you move here, but I can't promise you I will never do this again."

Right at that moment, I heard the Holy Spirit say to my spirit, "The covenant of your marriage is broken." I knew when I heard that in my spirit, I was free from this marriage. At the time, after two broken relationships, I had no desire to marry again or have a relationship with any man. No longer did I trust men; to me they were all alike. God knew I felt this way and knew it was wrong for His child to have such a distrust of a person because they were male. He knew this distrust would hinder me in ministry also. Before getting the position with the boys, I had tried to get a counseling job with girls, but that position wasn't open at the time. So even then, the Lord was trying to show me that I couldn't put all men in the same box. When you think about it, it did not make sense, because Jesus was male and so was my dad.

CHAPTER 18

Looking for Love the Right Way

After a few months went by, it kind of bothered me that I didn't have a partner to do things with, like going to church together. Really, I just wanted a friend and didn't want the intimate side of marriage. I became confused about my feelings. I knew I was free to marry as my husband had committed adultery many times and was unrepentant, and I had already been granted a divorce. I believe that's exactly what my husband wanted me to do, as he would be able to tell his mother that it was I who had divorced him. He even told the church people in our hometown that I had left him, though I didn't find this out until much later.

The Lord's Choice

So, in my lonely state, I began to wonder if I should marry again. I was still confused, so I asked God if He would show me if I should marry. If so I asked Him whether He would bring into my life within two weeks the man I would marry. I said, "Lord, I do not want to date anyone." Since my children were older, I didn't want to embarrass them either. Also, if He sent a man to me—even though I thought it was impossible—the man would have to be faithful and never think of being unfaithful. I was really trying to make it as hard as possible for the Lord to bring me someone. There was no way I would get involved with another man, unless I knew with absolute certainty it was the Lord's will and choice for me.

He would have to be a man of prayer, like Daniel in the Bible. I also told the Lord that my dad was the last faithful man on earth. I know you think that is silly, but I had chosen two men to marry, two very different men. I had chosen these men without the guidance of God because I was not a child of God at the time and didn't realize that the Lord should be in my decisions. I knew this time that it would have to be the Lord who chose my marriage partner if I were to ever marry again. How many times had I counseled young people with the same advice?

To my amazement I met the man God wanted me to marry within the two weeks. He also fulfilled every other request I had made to my Father in heaven.

My middle daughter actually knew the man God would bring into my life. She had dated his stepson in high school for a short while and, even though they were no longer dating, she had remained friends with him. So, I was introduced to my future husband by his stepson, who told me his mother had left his dad for another man and had remarried. This would be her third marriage, and my husband and my third marriage too. The similarities and experiences in relationships between my husband, Jerry, and I were astounding.

He had married in his second year of college, had two beautiful daughters; then, his wife had left him and moved out of state, and devastated him by taking his children away. Jerry's brother, mother, and father were living in another state, so in his loneliness, he moved to be close to them. He didn't want to follow his ex-wife because he couldn't handle what she was doing and was still angry. In this new state he met a woman with two sons who was also divorced. Jerry married her and took over the role of father to them. His girls also spent time with him in the summers.

With his second wife and two sons, after twenty years of marriage, he came home one day to find a note on the kitchen table saying that she was leaving to be with a man she had met a year ago at work.

Again, he was devastated. He tried to get her to come to counseling, but she told him and the counselor in just one session that she loved Jerry but would not give up the other man. The counselor said that you can't love two men the same way in a marriage. That was the end of the counseling. She went on to marry the other man.

Jerry became very depressed, stopped eating, smoked three packs of cigarettes a day, and looked like a six-foot five-inch skeleton. He had lost so much weight that even though he was just in his late forties, he looked a lot older. It was in this time of depression that he would turn to God. His brother invited him to church, and he gave his heart to God. This is what he looked like and the condition of his heart when I first met him.

When I finally agreed to go out with him, he drove up to my apartment in a truck, which most South Georgian men that were hunters did. In fact, he loved the outdoors as much as I did. I got in and we had some small talk. Then he said, "I need to stop at the store for a minute."

I thought, "Uh oh. What's this about?" When he came out of the store, he had a loaf of bread in his hand. "What's that for?" I asked.

"It's for the ducks."

I was relieved. Like I said, I didn't trust men. He drove me to a small park with a pond full of ducks and we sat on a bench under a large oak tree on a warm sunny day with a slight breeze—my favorite kind of weather. We talked for hours while feeding the ducks.

As we talked, I was so conscious of the similarity between us. We had both grown up in the longer winters of Michigan and Indiana. We both had emotional pain from our younger years from one of our parents. For him, it was his father who criticized him. It's not easy being a parent without God in your life, and Jerry's parents, like mine, didn't seem to have room for God. Between us, we had been married for close to thirty-something years. We'd both intended to be married for life like our parents, but our partners had made decisions over which we had no control. Our marriage experiences had soured our attitude toward marriage and relationships. I didn't realize how deeply it affected Jerry until we married.

But we were married shortly after we met. We did not want a long dating period and felt God had brought us together so there wasn't much sense in waiting. I was so impressed by how sensitive and caring Jerry was about what I thought. He really listened and discussed things with me. He would also talk to his daughters on the phone every day, as both lived in different states. They would tell him everything and ask for his advice. I admired him so much as a father.

Being a brand-new believer, he knew nothing about God's word. In fact, when I first had a conversation with him, I could tell he had many worldly misconceptions about the God he had given his heart to. I had been a teacher of God's word for a long time and had experienced His presence in my life. The Lord knew what we both needed in our lives: to know Him better. For Jerry, it was to understand who God was through His word. One night, I had a dream in which the Lord spoke to me saying, "Your husband will be to you like one of your foster children. He has been crushed emotionally. Be patient with him just as you were with them."

I knew Jerry had been hurt but I didn't realize how much God would require me to be used for his healing. The beautiful thing was that he loved to study the Bible with me and didn't mind me teaching him. In fact, he devoured the word of God.

I soon began to see how deeply Jerry had been hurt and what the Holy Spirit meant by him being like one of my foster children. Whenever we would go out to eat or go to the mall, he would accuse me of looking at other men. Now, I'm a people person, so I look at everyone when I'm out, but never in my life, even in my other troubled marriages, did I ever think or look at another man with any interest beyond the platonic. I never had an unfaithful thought in my mind, even when my husbands were cheating. It got so bad when we got home that he would keep accusing me and we would get into arguments. I tried to defend myself. He would want to go out to eat often, but I started making excuses, so I didn't have to go. I began to think, "What have I gotten myself into? I can't stand this jealous spirit of his."

So I cried out to the Lord, "I can't take this, Lord. I would rather be alone the rest of my life than live like this."

Well, I really heard God loud and clear in this answer to my cry. "Who said you have to take it," He said.

"What do you mean?" I said.

"Dolores, why are you defending yourself? Is what he says about you true?"

"No," I said.

"The important thing is that I know you and what you think and, if you are right with Me, what does it matter what someone thinks about you? All through your life you felt you had to defend yourself, but all you were doing was reinforcing how the enemy was using that person to harm you. I cannot convict the one who is lying about you because of your arguing and trying to defend yourself. Your husband only hears your voice, not Mine."

After all these years, it was like a light bulb went on. That was exactly what I had done when I was young and in my marriages. I had finally gotten sick of the back and forth to really ask and listen to God's advice after almost thirty years of relationship problems in spite of walking with the Lord.

I told the Lord I was sorry for not being open to him sooner, "But how should I treat Jerry when he gets jealous and angry?"

He told me, "Jerry has been hurt and doesn't trust women, but I won't allow him to abuse you. When he starts to accuse you, tell him that you won't argue with him and that he needs to come to Me about it. Say to him, 'I know I'm not looking at men or unfaithful in any way. I'm alright with God, and He knows me.'" Then the Lord said I was to walk away.

So that's exactly what I did. Of course, it made Jerry mad at first that I wouldn't argue with him, and he would try his darndest by yelling at me to get me mad. But I was free for the first time in my life about what other people thought about me, especially those close to me. I really loved Jerry and had to learn not to care what he or anyone else thought. What mattered was that God loved me and He knew the truth. I could live without a husband, but I couldn't live without God in my life. The amazing thing was that after about three weeks of not responding to Jerry's jealousy, he stopped it. He would always go to his office angry—which was in our house—after I wouldn't respond to his accusations. He told me later that he would go and pray. You see, I knew God had sent me a Daniel when it came to prayer. Young as he was in the Lord, Jerry talked to God about everything.

Years later, my husband just one day out of the blue said, "Dolores, do you know why I stopped being jealous?"

"No, why?" I asked.

"It wasn't about how much you loved me. I knew you loved me, but I realized how much you love Jesus and would never be unfaithful to Him."

I thought that if we only would look for, listen, and obey God's instructions and advice instead of trying to handle things by ourselves, what a beautiful life we would have! But we human beings, saved by grace, and even devoted servants of God, will at times fall into the carnal ways we had learned from the world. So many times the carnal self wants to rule and take over control, even though we should be walking in God's Spirit. Our Father in heaven allows these tests and failures to remind us that our flesh is dead and doesn't have eternal life—only our spirit does. He leaves His born-again children on earth to be a light to the world, to lead people to Jesus, the Light. At the same time, He strengthens and matures us spiritually so that less and less will we be tempted by our sensual appetites.

Also, He is bringing us even to the point of being willing to die for the gospel. Knowing our Father's heart for us, we will never turn away from Him like Adam and Eve did. God allowed Jerry and me a couple of years to work out the kinks in our relationship and get to know each other better. I can't say everything was perfect, but it was close to it because we made the Lord the head of our home. In the end, being married to my husband was like having Jesus in a physical form in our home.

We would never argue. If we disagreed with one another, we no longer tried to defend our positions by being argumentative. Instead, we went to prayer separately to get God's guidance. Many times, I would go back to Jerry and tell him that he was right in a situation, and he would do the same with me. Many times, if the word "Sorry" needed to be said, it was said, because our Father in heaven had instructed us to. We did not make a decision without going to the Lord and coming into agreement.

CHAPTER 19

The Tug of Ministry

After the Lord had given us time to get to know each other, I began to feel the tug of ministry again. We were attending a local church, but we knew there were some of our friends who were Christians that had been attending the church my ex-husband and I had pastured, and they hadn't found another church. I had suggested a couple of churches to them that would meet their spiritual needs, but they still had not gone.

In the meantime, Jerry had a heart attack—the first one. The doctors said that he needed a heart bypass but because we didn't have medical insurance, the doctor changed his mind and sent my husband home with a change of diet. We did change his diet, but Jerry and I both knew that if his heart was so damaged that he needed bypass surgery, a diet would not heal his heart. And he was trying to give up smoking too but having a hard time.

As a young child of God, it was hard for Jerry to believe God would heal him and set him free of nicotine addiction. He hadn't had enough experience with God and His word. So, within six months, he had his second heart attack. He was rushed to the hospital to have a heart bypass. The cardiologist didn't want to do the operation because he said Jerry's heart was so bad that he would have to stop his heart to operate. He told us both he felt Jerry would not survive the operation.

That was very scary to hear, but we had prayed that, if the doctor was willing to operate, God was in control. So, we told him that we wanted him to operate. He agreed and they operated the next day. When the doctor came out, he said, "It's amazing—it went perfectly. He's not out of the woods yet and we'll know more in the morning."

Jerry was put into intensive care, and I wasn't allowed to see him. They told me I couldn't stay with him overnight. We had to go to Tallahassee for the operation, so I stayed in a motel near the hospital and the hospital staff said they would call me if there was a turn for the worse. So, I left thanking God that he was with my husband and would bring him through this. All the same I had a sleepless night. I couldn't wait to get back to the hospital. I arrived very early in the morning and the first thing I asked Jerry's nurse was how he was. She said, "His heart stopped during the night, but we got it started again."

"Why didn't you call me? What if he didn't recover?" I said.

"We didn't have time—everything happened so fast," she said. "The doctor will talk to you about it when he comes in."

She allowed me through to intensive care to see him. When I walked in, they had put a breathing tube down his throat, and he couldn't speak. The look in his eyes was pure terror; it was a look of "Please help me!" He wanted that breathing tube out of his throat. He told me later it was the worst experience of his life and he felt like he was choking on it all the time.

I felt so helpless. Here was a man I had learned to love and trust. He was hurting and I couldn't help him the way I wanted to. They had tied his hands down because he was trying to pull the tube out. Here was a six-foot-five gentle giant of a man, as others had called him, lying there in total fear. I was the only one there with him. The rest of the family, some living out of state, couldn't make it in time as they scheduled the operation so quickly. His daughters, brother and mother were able to come soon. While he was in the hospital, the doctor who had operated on him decided to have a defibrillator installed in his chest to combat Jerry's continuing heart palpitations.

If his heart stopped, the defibrillator would start it again. Thank God for that defibrillator because he only had twenty percent of his heart functioning and his heart would stop and start three more times in later years. Altogether, he'd had five heart attacks.

When we went back to my husband's cardiologist in Valdosta, he told me that Jerry would not last the year. He could no longer work, either, as it would be too stressful. Some of my relatives and Christian friends got together and we prayed about the situation. The idea came to me that maybe it would be a good idea to meet in my relatives' Steve and Denise's home for church for a while. It would also be easy for my husband and me to attend since they lived near us. They agreed and we started a house church in their home. The word got around quickly, and we had quite a few people coming.

We had a few people who were new believers and some who were not surrendered believers yet. We met together a couple of years with God doing many physical, emotional, and financial miracles among us and through us. After a couple of years, Jerry had another heart attack and his doctors put him on close to $1500 in prescription drugs. I kept praying that God would heal him, as did our house church members.

But Jerry couldn't seem to have faith that God would heal him completely. My brother-in-law, Steve, had been given a healing ministry by the Spirit of God, and had great faith in this area. Whenever my husband would have a heart episode and had to go to the hospital, the doctor would always say, "He won't make it out of the hospital." But Steve would go in, lay hands on Jerry, and pray that he'd get better and be released. For years, that's what happened.

After a few years, Jerry began to have trouble with fluid building up in his body, and the medicine wasn't helping. My oldest daughter and her husband had moved to Winston-Salem, North Carolina. After I told her I felt the doctors were giving him too much medication that wasn't helping him, she said, "Why don't you move here? They have a great hospital here specifically for heart problems, and the doctors are outstanding." It didn't hurt that she mentioned how much our grandkids missed us.

I didn't want to leave the church, but I knew it was in capable hands with some strong Christians there, who were also anointed for ministry. I also missed my oldest grandchildren. After much prayer, my husband and I felt we should move to North Carolina. It really was a God idea because the doctors there took my husband off half of his medicine, and he stopped being sick all the time. He felt well enough to work out in the little workshop outside the house we were renting, which he hadn't done in so long. We got to spend a lot of time with my children and our grandchildren.

We had been there for over a year and a half, but I was still keeping up with how the house church was doing in Valdosta through my former sister-in-law. At first, it was doing well, but after a while, a man who had begun to attend—and was a former Pastor—was doing most of the preaching. My sister-in-law, Denise, said they were beginning to have a little trouble because this man had a full-time job and wanted to pastor the house church but had to work some Sundays. On top of that, they were not allowed to share what the Holy Spirit was giving them as they had been used to. I began to pray about the situation.

I knew there were new Christians going there. If the enemy got into this small work, they would be hurt. The problem did not clear up, and after a while some of the members asked if my husband and I could come back. My husband's brother and mother still lived in Valdosta, and I knew that because of my daughter and her husband's business, they might have to move again. I began to feel that tug again on my spirit to get involved in ministry again.

I know a lot of Christians believe a woman is not called to be a Pastor. My understanding of the New Testament was that "elders" were the leadership and a Pastor was just one of the elders—so it wasn't one elder leading the church. I always felt God had used me to start these works, just as missionaries did in other countries. Then He would bring others who had a calling on their lives to help establish these ministries.

One day, one of the people from the house church called me and said that the man who had taken over as Pastor was not coming to the service on different Sundays because he could make double pay on his job if he worked on Sunday. They told him it would be fine with them and wished him well. I knew the people that attended there all had jobs and didn't feel called to full-time ministry. I also knew that God had called me to full-time ministry years ago. They didn't need one person to take over as Pastor, but they did need an elder who could be counted on to be there and be a sort of coordinator and bring together the other elders who were teachers, prophets, evangelists, and missionaries/apostles to operate in their calling as the Holy Spirit led.

I talked to my daughter and, although she hated to see us go, she knew God was calling us. It wasn't long before they too felt they were to move back to Michigan. The strange thing was that after living somewhere else, going back to South Georgia felt like I was coming home. I didn't feel that way about the state I was born in and lived for over twenty years.

When we got back, we stayed with my sister and brother-in-law for a while. Our funds were limited, and we knew that we couldn't afford much for rent, so we decided the best solution was to buy a used mobile home. We found an older double-wide model in good condition which sold for $8000. We went to the bank and asked for a $14,000 loan. We prayed as we had only the little I was paid for by the Ministry and the disability check Jerry received. We didn't even have any money to put down, or collateral for the loan. We prayed for God's favor, and they approved the full amount of the loan. We knew that most mobile homes at that age only sold for

$8000 to $10,000 at the most but we needed money to move it and remodel. We bought a piece of property on Denise and Steve's land, which they allowed us to make easy payments on, and moved our mobile home in.

Before I was a Christian, I would have thought I was too good to live in a mobile home, but now I was so thankful that God had provided us a place to live. It's amazing what a few years of doing things our way will teach us about being humble and thankful. Also, over the years God would not only provide a home for Jerry and me, but a way for me to care for him and pursue ministry at the same time.

Added to that my ex-sister-in-law, Denise, and her husband, Steve, lived just a block from us, and Steve was Jerry's best friend. He was always there to help Jerry when we needed him. And there were so many times this man of God was needed.

That first Sunday back at the Home Church was a joyous occasion. Everyone was so glad we were back, and we realized how much we had missed their worship. Things settled in; we made arrangements for a new cardiologist and primary physician for my husband. The primary physician was a young man just starting his practice, and over the years he would take excellent care of Jerry.

CHAPTER 20

Valdosta Coffee House Ministry

We would continue to meet at the house church for about six months. Those mostly attending were family and friends and I was happy with our small church family. Above all, it was convenient for my husband and me with his heart issues. We were both older, and even though the Lord had not told me I would never open another coffee house ministry again, I just looked at my circumstances and assumed that the ministry was done. Never assume anything with God especially by looking at impossible circumstances.

Stepping Out in Faith Again

One Sunday morning as I was getting ready for church, I turned on the TV to listen to another Christian ministry while getting ready. A woman, who I had listened to before, was teaching. I was aware God was using her to reach many people including some of my friends. When she taught, I knew it was coming from the Holy Spirit, because of my own study of the word. She always glorified God through

His Son, which of course was the work of the Spirit of God through her. As I was listening to her message, I began to think, "God are you speaking to me?"

Suddenly, I heard His voice loud and clear in my spirit, "You are not finished with the coffee house ministry. I am going to ask you to step out in faith again." He went on to tell me that He wanted me to open a coffee house ministry in Valdosta. It was so strong, and I knew His voice. I was so excited, I didn't question him.

That Sunday I told the people what God had said, I asked them to pray about it because God would have to open all the doors and provide the funds we didn't have. I told them God wanted to do more of an outreach by taking us into the marketplace. He wasn't just asking me to step out in this ministry again; He was asking them to be a part of it. Some at first were not too happy about adding more responsibility to our comfortable little fellowship, but they promised to pray.

By the next Sunday, we were all in agreement we would look for a building for the Café. Right away Steve mentioned an area by our university. Again, I was making assumptions instead of asking God. Since most of our church members were around forty and above, I assumed the ministry would be geared toward that age group, rather than college students. Because of my assumptions I would so many times miss God's big picture. Thank God, He didn't let me stay in that mindset long. I looked and looked on my own for a building, but nothing opened. Not only could we not afford the high rents in the city, but at that time there weren't many buildings available.

Finally, Steve—bless his heart—who was so patient with me, said, "Dolores, why don't you go to the area near the

College where all the small older homes have been made into retail shops?"

I thought, "Well, I guess I should go look; he seems to know something I don't." So, I drove over to the area he had suggested, not far from the university.

There were some quaint small South Georgian houses, reminiscent of earlier times with their long front porches, where people would sit and greet their neighbors as they walked by. Most were already occupied with small boutiques, restaurants, and gift shops; it was a perfect spot for retail. As I drove by, a sign in front of the building caught my eye. It said it was for rent and seemed to be the only building not occupied.

The house was so cute; it had been painted pink, with white shutters on the windows and a long white porch along the front of the house. When I called the number on the sign, the man that answered asked me to wait, and he came right over. He said he owned quite a few businesses in town. I loved the way the place had been decorated. It was bright with large front windows, and pastel colors that looked so pretty with the white brick fireplace. It only had one bathroom, but a large back room for a kitchen. It would be perfect for us, even though we wouldn't need the kitchen.

I explained to him that I wanted to open a coffee house ministry as a non-profit; rather than selling the coffee and donuts, we would just be accepting donations. He informed me the rent would be $1000 a month, the same that was charged by the other retail shop owners along this strip. I was a little shocked, expecting it to be $700-$800, which would have been too much for us anyway.

I told him that $1000 a month was too high for a non-profit. What I did not tell him is that my small church group had prayed and asked God what to pay for rent. Through the prayer the Lord said we were to pay $400 a month. We knew that we did not have any extra money to rent a building, and the Lord would be the one to provide. When I heard that amount, I knew God would have to perform a miracle, since rents for commercial property in Valdosta were so high.

I told the owner of the building the amount God had given us. He said," Oh no! I can't do it for that." I didn't offer any other amount nor did he. We parted without any further discussion. I was kind of discouraged, because I felt this building was the building God had chosen and would be perfect for the coffee house. I went home and prayed for guidance but wasn't getting any other direction. The next day I received a call from the owner of the building. He said he had thought it over and would be able to rent the building for $600, even though he would be losing money. As he was talking, I thought "Oh God, can't we do it for that amount? Does he have to come down to $400?" But I kept hearing, "I gave you $400 and that has not changed." So, I said, "I'm sorry, the Lord told us $400 is what we are to pay; we had all prayed about it."

He didn't speak for what seemed like a long time, and then said, "No, I can't do it. I have a partner and he wouldn't accept your offer." So, we ended the call.

I began to feel despair, until the Lord reminded me that, if He had called me to this work, then it was up to Him to bring it to pass. He again reminded me that this was His ministry not mine. "You're right, Lord, why am I worrying about something I have no resources or ability to bring about myself."

The next day I received a telephone call from the owner of the building. He said, "I've changed my mind, I'm going to allow you to rent the building for $400 a month. I feel I owe it to my grandmother who always talked to me about God when I was growing up. I'm doing this for her."

I was so excited and thought, "Lord, while I was starting to doubt You, You were working on this man's conscience to change his heart." I told the Lord how sorry I was for doubting Him. I knew He forgave me, and even though I had this brief period of doubt, He was working to answer the needs of the fellowship. I could have ruined it by entertaining the doubt that entered my mind, if not for God reminding me of who He was and what He had done in similar situations. With the trust He activated in my heart, He worked on that man until he submitted to Him. Only the Holy Spirit would have known the love he had for his grandmother, and could use it to change this man's mind.

Really it wasn't about the amount of money, because God could have provided the $1000 rent. After we opened, we received enough donations every month to go over that rental amount, but it had to do with being obedient to the Holy Spirit's leading instead of our own reasoning. The other part God had in mind for us was to help anyone in the fellowship and people that visited the coffee house who were in need. With many of the donations, we were able to do just that.

Meanwhile, our small congregation set to work fixing up a few things that were in disrepair, but otherwise the place was perfectly set up for a coffee house. The tables and chairs from the restaurant were still there, and we used the kitchen to keep supplies of paper products, coffee, tea, and children's drinks. We would pick up fresh pastries before opening every morning.

We had planned, like all outreach ministries, to be open during the week except Sunday and Monday. Friday nights would be a time of music and testimonies for the youth. A young man from the University agreed to oversee Friday nights and was very excited about having a place of fellowship for young people of different backgrounds. Saturday night was used as an outreach for older adults. We would be open during the week to anyone who just stopped by and wanted to study the Bible, or fellowship and, of course, there were those that were just curious to find out what we were all about. However, God didn't quite go along with all our plans.

There's a Christian song that says, "God left the ninety-nine to find that one that was lost." I believe a big reason the Lord called this particular coffee house ministry into being was largely about one person who was seeking him with all her heart. Her name was Jo Epling.

One day as I was working on our sign out front, trying to see if I could get the lights that Steve had installed to work, a young woman came running across the street from the building directly across from us. "Oh, praise God!" she said as she ran up to me. "Are you a Christian church or ministry?"

I was kind of taken back that she was so excited. I smiled and said, "Yes." She told me she had been praying that God would send someone to help her, as she had just become a Christian. She began to share a story with me about a friend of hers that was a nurse in our local hospital. One of her patients had a heart attack, and while he was there, he shared with her about a ministry he and his wife was starting. He said, "It was a café called "The Open Door." She asked her nurse friend, if she knew where the café could be found? The friend wasn't sure.

A few weeks went by, and one day as she was getting ready to open her business, she noticed me across the street working on the sign. The night before closing her business she noticed our sign said Open Door Coffee House.

"Hi! I'm Joann Epling," she said. "I own the business across the street. Everyone calls me Jo."

Being a new Christian, she was amazed by the things and circumstances God was bringing together for her, showing her how much He loved her. Not only would this young woman come alongside me in the coffee house Ministry, but I had the joy of watching her grow in Christ throughout the years. Every day she would witness to people who came to her business, and was used by the Holy Spirit to minister to people who came into the coffee house. She reminded me so much of myself; Jesus not only had saved her, but He had also put a fire in her bones to share the gospel with the lost. I knew He had called her into ministry, but she was still a babe in Christ. Our Father in Heaven had made me a spiritual mother to teach her God's ways, and He would have other mature Christians alongside her to mentor her.

When I said the Holy Spirit had called this coffee house ministry for one person, I didn't mean that others weren't touched by the Lord as well. But this woman would be prepared by God to—much later—be part of a ministry that went all over the world to preach the Gospel and bring help for people in disaster areas and refugees, who had been displaced by natural calamities, war and famine.

We could only fit forty-five people in our little café— anymore and the Fire Marshal would stop us from renting the building. It was hard when we first started because on our Friday or Saturday ministry nights, we had quite a few more than that, especially since we would ask music groups from different churches to come play instruments and worship. Sometimes people from those churches would attend also, which made it difficult to stay within the limit.

Our donations not only covered all our expenses, but we were able to help people with food, rent and utilities when needed. One of the families that came regularly had a car breakdown, and they had to walk all the way. A regular said he would be willing to fix their car, if they would buy the parts. As they were a poor family, the ministry stepped in and was able to buy the parts.

That was one of the things that I loved about small mission ministries. You became family and were aware of each other's needs, a lot of times without them even having to share. Sometimes in very large churches, your own members' needs might get looked over because you're so busy sending money to this ministry or that mission, or building larger buildings, to make room for more people. It might be better to mother new churches, and encourage other people called of God into ministry to lead these mission churches. Large numbers may indicate worldly success, but it doesn't necessarily mean success in God's eyes, especially if large parts of the fellowship are not having their spiritual and material needs met or their ministry callings used.

The Lord often used our little coffee house fellowship to pray for others that we knew who didn't attend our fellowship. One of our members was the ex-father-in-law of a man who was an alcoholic and was dying of alcohol poisoning. The man was in a coma, so we were asked to go to the hospital and pray for him. A few of the people from the fellowship went: the ex-son-in-law, Jo, Denise, and myself. The nurse had told Jo, she didn't see any hope for him and that he was close to death. When we got there, his wife was in the room, and she didn't seem to want to pray along with us but didn't mind us praying. We formed a circle around his bed and began to pray.

As we did, I felt led by God's Spirit to kneel by his ear, and pray into his ear. I held his hand. As we prayed for a few minutes asking God to spare him and heal him, he began to squeeze my hand. I looked at his eyes, but they were still closed; there was not even a flicker or any other movement in his body. I looked at the others and said, "He heard us; he squeezed my hand." They all began to praise God.

I was so excited I knew the Lord was answering our prayer. We left his side without any other sign of recovery. The next day the nurse friend of Jo's let us know that the man had regained consciousness and was recovering so rapidly, he might be sent home soon. We were all so overjoyed at the Lord's faithfulness to His word.

Days later he contacted the ex-son-in-law from our fellowship and told him that he had heard everything I was praying in his ear, and knew he was not going to die. He also said he knew it was God telling him so. Not only did he not die, but he was set free from alcoholism. We would continue to see so many people saved and set free from addictions, so many marriages healed, finances restored, physical healings, and young people being used and growing in the Lord. It was a very exciting time. Even though my husband had a heart condition, he enjoyed coming to the coffee house with his friends. I kept praying Jerry would believe God for a complete healing.

Jerry's Struggle

Before he had his first heart attack, we were visiting the church of a Pastor friend, when a woman we didn't know came up to my husband and said, "You will live and not die." Of course, at that time we had no idea what she was talking about, because Jerry had never been sick while we were married. But her word to him had come to pass, as through the many years, many doctors would say he would die within a short time.

We were now going into five years since his first heart attack, and I would always remind Jerry of the woman's word from God to him. However, the doctors were always so negative about his chances of survival; they were giving him so much medicine and telling him that was why he was still alive. He was brought up in a time where we were taught doctors were god-like and the only ones that could heal you. Even though in his short time as a Christian, seeing other people receive healing and miracles from the Lord, and knowing the Lord was keeping him alive, he still was afraid. The one positive thing was that he wasn't ready to die, so when he would have another heart attack, or fluid would build up in his body, he believed what we all prayed for him:

202

"He will live and not die." We all knew we were in a spiritual battle for my husband's health.

There was no question that he believed that Jesus had paid the price for his sins and that he would spend eternity with God the Father. We all have our limitations in what we believe God can and will do, and it's harder when the enemy would attack Jerry's body every time he began to feel better or stronger. He would then get discouraged, and question whether God wanted him to receive complete healing. It was hard for anyone, no matter how mature you are in the Lord, when your body is racked with pain or sickness. On the one hand your body is speaking death to you, and on the other, the Holy Spirit is reminding you of God's word and what He has done for you in the past.

Again, our relationship with God is based on faith. He can only do for us what we believe. Our pain and sickness are loud and unyielding, yet faith in God's word has no outward expression except what we confess with our mouth. So, it's a tussle between the belief to trust and choose what God says and what we feel in our screaming flesh. We also have a hard time during our trials in believing that our flesh has already died on the cross with Jesus. No longer are we under the curse of sin, or rulership of our flesh. We do not have to accept infirmity from the devil, nor do we have to accept any sickness or disease that afflicts our body. God wants us to speak His word to our flesh, just as Jesus spoke it to those who were crushed by sin. We can still speak it to those who are affected by curses on our land and environment caused by sin.

Too many times, when people do pray for healing, they expect it to happen all at once. When it doesn't, they assume God doesn't want to heal them. They believe the Lord's will is for them to remain sick and disabled or that God doesn't love them because He hasn't forgiven them. The truth is they haven't studied all the scripture about receiving healing—emotionally or physically. God's word teaches us that sometimes healing comes in stages. Because they do not know the full word of God, the enemy will tell them that they are not worthy of healing—which is of course a lie.

No one was ever worthy of what Christ's blood paid for. However, nowhere in scripture was anyone turned away without healing from Jesus, except by his own doubts. This happened in His own hometown, Nazareth: "Now he did not do many mighty works there because of their unbelief" (Matthew 13:58). These people had rejected who Jesus was, and in so doing rejected His power to heal them. It is very sad that they would stay in that condition when the Holy Spirit could bring faith to someone who is struggling, just as He did with the man who said to Jesus, "Lord I believe; help my unbelief."

God knows the constant struggle between the spirit and the flesh, but if we are willing, He will help us overcome our flesh. The Lord wants us to be persistent in our trust in His word, no matter how we feel, or what we see, or hear, or how long it takes. The life of the children of God doesn't depend on what the world taught us, for we are no longer a part of this cursed dying world. Instead, we depend on and believe every word that comes out of the mouth of God.

Have I always done this? No. When I 've been faced with circumstances, including my own sickness and pain, I have struggled every time. But Jesus has won the victory. The Holy

Spirit reminds me of what Jesus taught and did. He taught me that the Father has unconditional love and forgiveness for me. Even though I had rejected Him for so long, He showed me His great love and forgiveness for me by His sacrifice of Himself for me on the cross. Because of that, I choose to believe the Word of God, no matter what satan whispers to me or how my flesh feels, and I have received healing and victory every time.

My husband continued to have problems with his heart and, because he had a hard time exercising, he developed gout. I knew it was getting more difficult for him to go to the coffee house much as he wanted to be there. It was very tiring for him, and he had no place to lie down when he needed to. But I could not leave him at home alone. I began asking God what I should do. Should I close the coffee house ministry or maybe turn it over to someone else? Although, at the time, I didn't feel there was anyone, the Holy Spirit was showing me to do just that.

A New Church Building

After a few weeks of praying, I knew the Lord was leading me to close the café, but I felt He was also telling me not to close the ministry. I thought the only way I could continue was to go back to meeting as a home church. The only problem was we lived out in the country on a dirt road that, when the weather was bad, was hard to travel down. Plus, our mobile Home was not large enough for all the people who still wanted to be a part of our fellowship. We had quite a few men who wanted to stay in our fellowship that worked for, or owned construction companies and they suggested we construct a building on our one acre property for a church house.

We all prayed about it, and I had suggested they build it near the main paved highway leading out to our house. But after prayer the men said it would defeat the purpose of wanting my husband to come to the meetings, and when he needed to rest, he could go next door to our mobile home. It also would allow me more flexibility for ministry and meeting my husband's needs.

It's amazing how fast this building came together. Manpower and building materials were supplied by people in our fellowship, companies, and people we knew but were not a part of our ministry. The men and some of the women worked after their jobs and on weekends to finish it. The finished product was a cute one-thousand-two-hundred square-foot building with a canopy connecting the building to the mobile home. Eventually, they would add a slide for children and a large deck off the building for the fellowship to meet outside when there was nice weather. My husband had his own construction company when he worked and had designed many of his building projects. He did a great job with the canopy. Two of my relatives, Greg and Steve, who also had a construction company, oversaw and worked on the project. God had put the right people in our fellowship in this new home church. A few hotels were selling their custom upholstered chairs cheap enough for thirty-five people plus two couches.

We dedicated our house church, praising God for what He had accomplished. The bad dirt road didn't hinder people from coming. Some of the men would come an hour early to have coffee and fellowship together before service.

We had one problem though; we didn't have a worship leader. We had a nice electric keyboard we had used at the coffee house, but no one to play it. We had depended on young people who were musicians and worship leaders from other churches to play at the coffee house on Friday and Saturday nights in Valdosta, but the ministry at the café didn't have its own worship leader. After much prayer the Lord sent us one of the best worship leaders I've ever heard. God doesn't care whether you're a large or small church; He's going to give you His anointed best if you pray and believe.

This young girl had a beautiful voice and could play the piano. But she was blind from birth—we called her our female Ray Charles. She could have easily sung for the entertainment industry and made a lot of money; but she loved the Lord and wanted to sing for Him. On top of all that her mother, who was not a Christian would drive her daughter all the way for her to lead our worship. I have no idea why she chose our small fellowship, except that she listened to the Lord, and wanted to do His will.

When we started our service, we would sometimes pray for a long while, as well as for people who had sent us requests. At other times we would start with worship led by the Holy Spirit. As we waited on Him, He would speak to us through the Body of Christ with the gifts He gave them. Many times, He gave us words of wisdom or knowledge or prophetic messages, or tongues and their interpretation reminding us of what Jesus had said, and always correcting, edifying and building up our faith in the Lord God Almighty.

One of the outstanding miracles we witnessed was to an older man, named Robert, who attended our fellowship.

Robert had been an alcoholic most of his life and had come close to death many times through accidents. He also had lung and heart issues. He had accepted the Lord as a young child but had backslid years ago. After coming to the Open Door Café and house church, he rededicated his life to God. One time he told us how God had called him to the ministry as a young adult, but instead he had got caught up in partying and drinking. Now it was too late, he said. Almost everyone told him, "It's never too late with God," but he just smiled.

A couple of months later, during worship at a Saturday night meeting, there was a word of knowledge for Robert. "Robert it's not too late for you to minster the word of God. I'm calling you now to teach My word to the people. What you think is impossible, I have made possible." Three weeks later, I felt led to ask Robert to speak at our next meeting. He agreed, read scripture out of the Bible at that meeting, and continued to be one of our teaching elders.

What was so miraculous about this was that Robert couldn't read. He had quit school at an early age, worked in construction, and never felt the need to learn. Any reading he could do was elementary and He couldn't articulate words well. But Robert believed God's word to him, and went home, picked up his Bible, prayed, and found he could read the Bible. He would come to church and read the word of God to us as a part of a teaching or sermon he gave. He was overjoyed that God could forgive him for the years he'd wasted, and still love and use him.

We saw many healings, deliverances, and people surrendering to God at this small fellowship as people prayed for them. We believed God had given us the authority to use the name of Jesus Christ against anything that came against the promises of God. Matthew 17:20 says, "Even if you have the faith of a mustard seed and say to this mountain to move from here to there, it will move, and nothing will be impossible to you." In other words, "Even though you have little faith, if you believe with the little faith, you have and don't doubt, you will receive your answer."

This is not easy because we are taught to harbor so much doubt throughout our lives. We believe according to how our bodies feel, we believe the doctor, we believe other people's negative talk; we believe everything but the Lord God. I have been healed many times by the Lord both emotionally and physically. There are times I have had to wait for it, and this is when the father of lies (satan) is right there whispering in my ears, "What if you're not healed? What if you're going to die? Maybe God doesn't heal everyone, or maybe God doesn't exist. Or if He does exist, He doesn't care about you or love you because you're too bad and have disappointed Him."

What is absurd is satan will still try to cast doubts in my mind, no matter all the miracles, and answered prayer to God's promises I've experienced. What is even more absurd is when I'm faced with any kind of trial, my soulish reaction is doubt. But thank God for His Holy Spirit who always reminds us of who God is, who His Son is and His sacrificial love for us.

Just because you are having a hard time believing for the gift of healing, doesn't mean you haven't received the gift of salvation through your faith in Christ. Salvation through the blood of Christ comes through His sacrifice for you and nothing else. It doesn't come from how much faith you have in whether you get answers to your prayers, or signs and supernatural signs you see. It comes from faith alone that you are saved by Jesus' sacrificial death on the cross. That is your only door to heaven, not whether the healing of your body was manifested or not.

Does it grieve the Lord when we don't believe Him when His will is for us to have abundant life here on earth, which includes health? Yes, it does. Remember when the disciples couldn't cast the demon out of the man's young son that had caused the son to be mute and deaf, and threw him into the fire? Jesus was disappointed in the disciples' lack of faith, but He did not give up on them; instead, He told them that this demon, could only be cast out through prayer and fasting.

Remember our corrupted flesh will not enter heaven, neither will any of our carnal needs and lust. God will give us a new body and restore everything like it was before sin came into the world. God's will for us is to be totally healed and restored—body, soul, and spirit. Even Job, who was severely tested by satan was eventually healed, and God restored to him everything satan had stolen. The woman who had the issue of blood for twelve years, came up to Jesus and touched the hem of His garment, because she just believed, if she could touch Him, she would be healed. She never gave up for twelve years looking for healing, even after going from doctor to doctor, and spending all her money. After all those years looking in all the wrong places for her healing, trying all her own methods, which failed, she still never gave up wanting and believing she could be healed. When she finally realized she just needed Jesus, the Messiah, and He had the power to heal her, her faith caused it to happen.

The Word of God says in Hebrews 11:6, "But without faith it is impossible to please Him: for he that comes to God must believe that He exists, and He rewards those who earnestly seek Him." Our God not only exists, but He rewards us by bringing to pass His promises to us in this life and in the life to come.

CHAPTER 21

Goodbye, Brother or Sister

I'm writing my testimony, first of all, because the Lord asked me to. Secondly, I want people to see that Jesus is still walking the earth through the Holy Spirit who is dwelling in believers. He is still reaching out to the "poor in spirit," and the emotionally and physically crushed. He's still offering what He did on the cross for man's sins, still promising eternal life to those that believe in Him, still warning of eternal damnation for those who choose not to believe in Him.

I'm writing this to show that once we have committed our lives to Jesus Christ, God becomes our Father and we become His newborn children. He begins to raise us up, giving us a heart that pleases Him, teaching us His ways, and getting rid of all the lies this sinful world has taught us. He shows us how Jesus defeated satan who held us in bondage, He forgives us when we fall into temptation, He gives when we ask Him, and helps us grow us in our faith and trust of Him, and in the fruit of the Spirit. All this is a demonstration of the light of Christ in our lives to draw others to the cross. It takes away every strategy of satan to turn humankind towards worshiping him instead of God. But Jesus ended all satan's lust for power on the cross. Now mankind is free of satan's bondage, just by accepting Christ's payment for their sin. Soon satan and those that choose to believe in his lies and follow him, will go to the place God prepared for the devil and his rebellious angels. Then all God's children will receive new bodies, and God's kingdom will be established here on earth.

Because God is love, He wants to give us a second chance to believe Him instead of satan's lies, and not make the choice Adam and Eve did. Real Love is always a choice: it cannot be forced. And God wants us to love Him and live with Him forever.

I know there are some who won't believe some of these supernatural experiences I've written about. These are people who do not believe what was recorded for us and inspired by the Holy Spirit in God's word. Some won't believe because they believe in a God they have fabricated for themselves, a God who has no power. Some won't believe because they are afraid to get out of the boat and walk on the water to Jesus. Fear and faith cannot work in the same space.

I'm also writing my story to show how faithful God is to us, and how we can do nothing without him. It is **He** that begins the work in us, and it is **He** that will bring us to the finish line. In the last fifty some years, God kept His promise to me about my parents who gave their hearts to Jesus very late in life. My brother believed and prayed on his death bed, and God sent him a vision to help him through, "the valley of the shadow of death." My two ex-husbands prayed and repented before they died. My third husband lived over ten years past the death pronouncements made over him by the doctors. He grew so close to the Lord in the last year of his life, that he didn't want us to pray for him, because he wanted to be home with Jesus. The medicine the doctors gave him was causing his kidneys to fail, so he kept battling with water build up. What was so amazing was that he chose his day of death. God not only granted it, but spoke to me in the middle of the night and told me I was not to pray for my husband, because He was going to take him home with Him: and it happened that very hour. What was sad was that all the heart trouble did not cause his death. It was the fluid retention medication that finally stopped working, and had destroyed his kidneys. I hated to lose his kindness and warmth. After all that I had experienced with men, he changed my attitude towards men.

All three of my daughters and sons-in-law are walking with Jesus and sharing the Gospel. All my children and grandchildren are being blessed and favored by the Lord. My sister and her family are also walking with God. Satan had tried to kill her at different times, but God shielded her just as He did me. She has been a real light in her church and mission work. Her work was in a section of the city that is very poor, dangerous and drug-infested. The many people rescued by that mission are grateful for God's help through her. Many of my older friends that were part of the Christian coffee houses we opened have gone to heaven but younger people are still carrying on God's work. My friend and former sister-in-law, Denise, and her husband, Steve, are still serving the Lord through their local church. My friend JoAnn who came running across the road to the Open Door Café, served many years on the mission field, and is now at home still serving the Lord.

One day I will join all these people before the throne of God, because "God so loved the world that He gave His only begotten Son, that whoever believes in Him shall not perish, but have eternal life."

My story and the road God is leading me down is not finished yet. The Holy Spirit has revealed many things to come to me about myself, my family and the people of this earth. I know that my journey on earth won't be long now; yet I will always live on. My spirit cannot die, so I will join those that went before me, and we will return to earth with the King of kings and the Lord of lords.

My prayer is that you will be with me in this glorious moment. I hope you will see in this book, how God could take an ordinary little girl, who really messed up her life in the early years, and patiently waited till she got sick and tired of trying to run her own life, until she found she didn't need anyone else but God. He waited for me, because He loved me and knew how much I needed Him.

For my life and my story, all Glory and Honor to the Father, to Jesus Christ the Son, and to the Holy Spirit, my Comforter and Friend!